Jesus

JOHN MACARTHUR, JOHN ELDREDGE, MAX LUCADO,

CHARLES R. SWINDOLL, SHEILA WALSH, BILLY GRAHAM,

DEE BRESTIN AND KATHY TROCCOLI, ANNE GRAHAM LOTZ

W PUBLISHING GROUP
A Division of Thomas Nelson Publishers
Since 1798
www.wpublishinggroup.com

Published by W Publishing Group, a Division of Thomas Nelson, Inc., P.O. Box 141000, Nashville, Tennessee 37214.

Produced with the assistance of The Livingstone Corporation: www.LivingstoneCorporation.com. Project staff includes Greg Asimakoupoulos, Linda Taylor, Mary Horner Collins, and Dave Veerman.

All Scripture quotations, unless otherwise indicated, are taken from the New King James Version (NKJV®). Copyright © 1982 by Thomas Nelson, Inc. Used by permission. All rights reserved.

Other Scripture quotations are taken from the following sources:

The Holy Bible, New Century Version (NCV). Copyright © 1987, 1988, 1991 by W Publishing, Nashville, Tennessee. Used by permission. The New American Standard Bible (NASB), © 1960, 1977 by the Lockman Foundation. The New American Standard Bible® (NASBU). Copyright © 1960, 1962, 1963, 1968, 1971, 1972, 1973, 1975, 1977, 1995 by The Lockman Foundation. Used by permission. The HOLY BIBLE, NEW INTERNATIONAL VERSION® (NIV). Copyright © 1973, 1978, 1984 by the International Bible Society. Used by permission of Zondervan Bible Publishing House. All rights reserved. The "NIV" and "New International Version" trademarks are registered in the United States Patent and Trademark Office by International Bible Society. Use of either trademark requires the permission of the International Bible Society. The *Holy Bible*, New Living Translation (NLT), copyright © 1996. Used by permission of Tyndale House Publishers, Inc, Wheaton, Illinois 60189. All rights reserved. The Amplified Bible (AMP). Old Testament copyright © 1965, 1987 by The Zondervan Corporation. The Amplified New Testament copyright © 1958, 1987 by The Lockman Foundation. Used by permission.

This book is a compilation from previously published works and, therefore, contains various writing and editorial styles; however, those styles have been retained out of respect for the authors whose works we have graciously been given permission to include.

Library of Congress Cataloging-in-Publication Data

Jesus.
    p.cm.
Includes bibliographical references (p. 176) and index.
ISBN 0-8499-1834-0
    1. Jesus Christ--Meditations.
BT203.J468 2004
232--dc22

2004017374

Printed in the United States of America
04 05 06 07 08 PHX 9 8 7 6 5 4 3 2 1

Contents

ℒℴ

Introduction

ℜ

Jesus.

Through the centuries he has been written about, spoken about, and sung about more than any man in human history. He was a carpenter from Nazareth turned itinerant preacher—but so much more. A good man, even considered sinless, he was a great teacher who seemed to stir up controversy everywhere he went. But those who follow him and believe him to be the Son of God and Savior of the world know that Jesus was that—and still much more. As he walked on earth and continues to strengthen lives today, those who call themselves Christian know him in innumerable ways.

He's our

- Lord
- Friend
- Healer
- Lover of our souls

- Mighty Warrior
- Teacher
- Prince of Peace
- Savior

This book explores these eight major attributes of Jesus to help give a fuller understanding of the depth and breadth of his personality and how he relates to us today. Each chapter, corresponding to one of these eight characteristics, includes an introduction followed by an excerpt from a book by one of today's top Christian authors as he or she discusses that aspect of Jesus' character.

In the chapter on Jesus as Lord, you'll read from John MacArthur, one of today's foremost Bible teachers. John MacArthur is pastor-teacher of Grace Community Church in Sun Valley, California, teacher on the international daily radio program *Grace to You,* and president of The Master's College and Seminary. His insights, taken from four of his books, help to discern the importance of understanding and personally accepting the lordship of Jesus.

John Eldredge, author of many books (including *Sacred Romance* and *Wild at Heart*), brings his insights on spiritual warfare from his book *Waking the Dead* to the chapter on Jesus as Mighty Warrior. The excerpt from his book reveals that the battle we face each day comes from a very real source and needs our very real Warrior to fight with us.

The chapter on Jesus as Friend includes a section from Max Lucado's book *Next Door Savior.* Max Lucado is minister for the Oak Hills Church in San Antonio, Texas, and a best-selling Christian author. You'll enjoy reading his insights into Jesus' desire to meet you right where you are.

Charles Swindoll is president of Dallas Theological Seminary and host of the nationally syndicated radio program "Insight for Living." His insights on Jesus as Teacher, drawn from his book *Simple Faith,* encourage us as we look at Jesus' teaching style and his ability to make tough truths easy to understand.

Sheila Walsh, a speaker with the Women of Faith conferences, has personally experienced Jesus as her Healer. In the excerpt from her book *The Heartache No One Sees,* Sheila is transparent as she shares her personal battle with depression and how Jesus helped her through it. She encourages us with words from Scripture and from experience about Jesus' healing power, no matter what illness we may face.

Everyone wants peace, but the only place to find true and lasting peace is in a relationship with Jesus, the Prince of Peace. In this section from his book *The Key to Personal Peace,* Billy Graham describes our quest for peace and tells us how to find it.

In their book *Falling in Love with Jesus,* Dee Brestin and Kathy Troccoli bring to life the concept of Jesus as Lover of our souls. Dee, author and Bible teacher, and Kathy, singer and songwriter, tell parts of their personal stories on their journey of discovering the vast and unimaginable love Jesus has for us.

Finally, Anne Graham Lotz, speaker and author, closes the book with her vivid description of Jesus, the Savior. The excerpt from her book *Just Give Me Jesus* reveals the Old Testament plan for salvation and the fulfillment of that plan in Jesus, who was the perfect sacrifice to take away sin, the one and only Savior.

After each excerpt, we have included a section written with you in mind. What does it mean that Jesus is *your* Lord, *your* Teacher, *your* Savior? This section helps to personalize the reality of Jesus' various roles in your life.

Each chapter also includes several key Bible verses on the topic, words from a great hymn of the faith that focuses on the topic, and questions for further thought.

This book is designed with several uses in mind. Personal reading, study of Scripture, and personal reflection on each topic will give you a new appreciation for Jesus and all he has done and continues to do for you. It can also be used in a small group study or in a Sunday school class. Focusing on one characteristic of Jesus each week, your small group can study the readings, look up the Scripture references, and discuss the questions.

In addition, we have provided a Bible reading plan that includes fifty-two weeks of readings to help you study Jesus' life and ministry in one year. This also could be adapted in any number of ways for small group study. Finally, a Scripture index gives you the key Bible verses used in this book.

All of these tools have been designed to bring the multifaceted personality of Jesus into focus in a way never before accomplished. We hope you enjoy the insights you'll receive about Jesus as you read this book. More than that, we hope Jesus becomes even more real to you—as your Lord, your Mighty Warrior, your Friend, your Teacher, your Healer, your Prince of Peace, the Lover of your soul, and your Savior.

—The Publisher

Jesus, the Lord

FEATURING THE WRITING OF JOHN MACARTHUR

There are as many opinions about Jesus as voices to express them. Not every opinion about the first-century carpenter-turned-rabbi is grounded in reality, however. Many times what is presented about Jesus is inconsistent with the Bible.

While some participants in the cultural debate on the identity of Jesus Christ may not doubt his existence, they will gladly relegate him to the category of influential prophet or charismatic (but misguided) teacher. Those in this camp are quick to praise his message of love and forgiveness, affirm his treatment of social outcasts, and cheer his nonmaterialistic lifestyle. But somehow, they ignore some of the things Jesus said about himself—unmistakable claims to divinity:

"All things have been delivered to Me by My Father, and no one knows the Son except the Father. Nor does anyone know the Father except the Son, and the one to whom the Son wills to reveal Him." (Matthew 11:27)

Again the high priest asked Him, saying to Him, "Are You the Christ, the Son of the Blessed?" Jesus said, "I am. And you will see the Son of Man sitting at the right hand of the Power, and coming with the clouds of heaven." (Mark 14:61–62)

"I and My Father are one." (John 10:30)

"You call me Teacher and Lord, and you say well, for so I am." (John 13:13)

"Whoever has seen me has seen the Father." (John 14:9 NVC)

Because many people find Jesus' claims to be controversial and explosive, they are limited in the ways they respond. If they aren't willing to accept him as equal with God, they must explain away what the Bible says, explain away his own words about himself, or attempt to pick and choose what they want to believe. Yet, Jesus did not leave us those options. As one person said in wise simplicity, "If Jesus is not Lord of all, he is not Lord at all." To paraphrase the observation made by C. S. Lewis, when you consider Jesus' statements about himself, you either have to believe he was telling the truth and that he is Lord, or you have to believe he was a madman. You don't have any other choice.

Coming to terms with Jesus' identity is a decision every person must make, for that decision has eternal ramifications. You either acknowledge Jesus is the Lord or you don't. There is no in-between.

In the following readings, John MacArthur explains what it means for us to accept Jesus as Lord. He says, "The choice we all make is this: either we're good enough on our own, through our belief system and morality, to make it to heaven; or we're not, and we have to cast ourselves on the mercy of God through Christ to get there. Those are the only two systems of religion in the world. One is a religion of human merit; the other recognizes that we find true merit in Christ alone, and it comes to the sinner only by grace." That choice makes all the difference.

READINGS FROM JOHN MACARTHUR

JESUS CHRIST, GOD AND MAN

Jesus Christ had to be more than a man; He also had to be God. If Jesus were only a man, even the best of men, He could not have saved believers from their sin. If He were even the right man from the seed of David, but not God, He could not have withstood the punishment of God the Father at the cross and risen from the dead. He could not have overcome Satan and the world but would have been conquered as all men are conquered.

If there was ever any question that Jesus was the Son of God, His resurrection from the dead should end it. He had to be man to reach us, but He had to be God to lift us up. When God raised Christ from the dead, He affirmed that what He said was true.

As clearly as the horizon divides the earth from the sky, so the resurrection divides Jesus from the rest of humanity. Jesus Christ is God in human flesh.[1]

JESUS CHRIST, HUMAN AND DIVINE

The humanity and deity of Christ is a mysterious union we can never fully understand. But the Bible emphasizes both.

Luke 23:39–43 provides a good example. At the cross, ". . . One of the criminals who were hanged blasphemed Him, saying, 'If You are the Christ, save Yourself and us.' But the other, answering, rebuked him, saying, 'Do you not even fear God, seeing you are under the same condemnation? And we indeed justly, for we receive the due reward of our deeds; but this Man has done nothing wrong.' Then he said to Jesus, 'Lord, remember me when you come into Your Kingdom.' And Jesus said to him, 'Assuredly, I say to you, today you will be with me in Paradise.'"

In His humanness, Jesus was a victim, mercilessly hammered to a cross after being spat upon, mocked, and humiliated. But in His deity, He promised the thief on the cross eternal life, as only God can.[2]

JESUS AS LORD: WHAT IT MEANS TO US

Take Up the Cross. In Matthew 10:32, Jesus talked about confessing Him as Lord and Savior: "Therefore whoever confesses Me before men, him I will also confess before My Father who is in heaven." And then in verses 34–36: "Do not think that I came to bring peace on earth. I did not come to bring peace but a sword. For I have come to 'set a man against his father, a daughter against her mother, and a daughter-in-law against her mother-in-law; 'and 'a man's enemies will be those of his own household.'"

It's not a friendly invitation; it's a warning: If you come to Christ, it may make your family worse, not better. It may send a rift into your family, the likes of which you have never experienced before. If you give your life to Jesus Christ, there will be an im-passable gulf between you and people who don't give their lives to Him. In fact, as the New Age Hindu mystic Deepak Chopra said to me on CNN Television: "You and I are in two different universes." I replied that he was exactly right. And that is not just true for strangers but also for family members, creating a severe breach in those most intimate of all relationships.

Verse 37 adds, "He who loves father or mother more than Me is not worthy of Me. And he who loves son or daughter more than Me is not worthy of Me." If you're not willing to pay the price of a permanent split in your family unless your loved ones come to Christ—if you're not willing to pay the price of greater trauma, greater conflict, greater suffering in your family—then you're not worthy to be Jesus' disciple.

Verse 38: "And he who does not take his cross and follow after Me is not worthy of Me." Wait a minute. In Jesus' time, people associated a cross with one thing and one thing alone: a cross was an instrument of death. He was saying that if you're not willing to have conflict with the world to the degree that it could cost you your life, then you're not worthy of Him.

Verse 39: "He who finds his life will lose it, and he who loses his life for My sake will find it." This is an echo of Luke 9. It's about losing your life. It's not a man-centered theology, it's a Christ-centered theology that says, "I give everything to Christ, no matter what it costs me, even if it costs me my life.". . .

Walk the Narrow Way. There's a common misconception that the choice between Christ and false gods is the choice between desiring to go to hell and desiring to go to heaven. I've heard preachers say the narrow way is the way of Christianity that people choose when they want to go to heaven, and the broad way is the way people choose who are content to go to hell. But they are misinformed or confused. It is not a contrast between godliness and Christianity on one hand and irreligious, lewd, lascivious pagan masses headed merrily for hell on the other. It is a contrast between two kinds of religions, both roads marked "This Way to Heaven." Satan doesn't put up a sign that says, "Hell—Exit Here." That's not his style. People on the broad road think that road goes to heaven.

It's also a contrast between divine righteousness and human righteousness, between divine religion and human religion, thus between true religion and false religion. God's Word described the Pharisees' problem in Luke 18:9, which says that they "trusted in themselves that they were righteous." It was a religion of human righteousness. They worshiped themselves. And that was inadequate, because they weren't righteous enough to meet the high standard of God's kingdom. Only Jesus can do that.

The choice we all make is this: either we're good enough on our own, through our belief system and morality, to make it to heaven; or we're not, and we have to cast ourselves on the mercy of God through Christ to get there. Those are the only two systems of religion in the world. One is a religion of human merit; the other recognizes that we find true merit in Christ alone, and it comes to the sinner only by grace. There may be a thousand different religious names and terms, but only two religions really exist. There is the truth of divine accomplishment, which says God has done it all in Christ, and there is the lie of human achievement, which says we have some sort of hand in saving ourselves. One is the religion of grace, the other the religion of works. One offers salvation by faith alone; the other offers salvation by the flesh.

Man-made and demon-designed systems of religion are based on the assumption that we don't really need a Savior, or aren't fully dependent on Him, because we have the capacity to develop our own righteousness. Just let God give us a little religious environment to aid our natural goodness, dispense a little power to us, or infuse a little strength into us. Give us a few rules, a few religious routines and rituals, and we'll crank up salvation on our own. The lie of human achievement comes under myriad different titles, but it's all the same system, because it's spawned out of the same source: Satan himself. He packages it in different boxes, but it's all the same product. On the other hand, the truth of divine accomplishment is Christianity. And it stands alone.

Tragically, most of humanity is religiously speeding down the wide highway of human achievement, convinced it's headed toward some fabulous heavenly destiny because of its own basic goodness, noble works, and religious deeds. By contrast, Jesus said the only true way to heaven is the narrow pathway of trusting Him alone as Lord and Savior. . . .

In Matthew 7:13–14, Jesus mentioned the narrow gate twice and the wide gate once. From the intersection, both roads look as if they lead to salvation. Both promise the pathway to God, to the kingdom, glory, blessing, heaven. But only one of the roads really goes there. The other is paved with self-righteousness as a substitute for the perfect righteousness God demands in Matthew 5:48: "Therefore you shall be perfect, just as your Father in heaven is perfect." Either you accept the truth that salvation comes from what God has done for you in Christ, or you will be left with nothing but your own sinful self-righteousness.

The main characteristic of the way of life Jesus pointed to was its narrowness. The broad way had all kinds of tolerance for sin, for laws beyond the law of God, and standards below and beyond the standards of God. Every man-made religious system is part of the scenery of the broad way. But Jesus didn't look for ways to compromise. He simply said, "You've got to get off that broad road. You must enter this narrow way. If you're going to be in the kingdom, you've got to come on these terms."

It is not enough to listen to preaching about the gate; it is not enough to respect the ethics; you've got to walk through the gate. And you can't come unless you abandon your self-righteousness, see yourself as a beggar in spirit, mourning over sin, meek before a holy God, not proud and boastful, hungering and thirsting for righteousness, and not believing you have it. Hell will be full of people who thought highly of the Sermon on the Mount. You must do more than that. You must obey it and take action.

You can't stand outside and admire the narrow gate; you've got to drop everything and walk through it. There's that self-denial again. You come through, stripped of everything. But isn't that narrow-minded? Does that mean Christianity doesn't allow room for opposing viewpoints? No compassionate tolerance? No diversity?

That's exactly right. We don't do it that way because we're selfish or prideful or egotistical; we do it that way because that's what God said to do. If God said there were forty-eight ways to salvation, I'd preach and write about all forty-eight of them. But there aren't: "Nor is there salvation in any other, for there is no other name under heaven given among men by which we must be saved," Acts 4:12 reminds us, no other name but Jesus.

In John's gospel, Jesus said, "I am the bread of life" (6:35); "I am the way, the truth, and the life" (14:6); "He who does not enter the sheepfold by the door . . . is a thief and a robber. . . . I am the door" (10:1, 7). Paul affirmed these words in 1 Timothy 2:5: "For there is one God and one Mediator between God and men, the Man Christ Jesus." There's only one: Christ and Christ alone. That's a narrow viewpoint. But that is Christianity. And it is the truth. You have to enter on God's terms, through God's prescribed gate. Christ is that gate. Holy God has the right to determine the basis of salvation, and He has determined that it is Jesus Christ and Him alone. You can enter only through Him, by faith. . . .

To come through the narrow gate, you must enter with your heart repentant over sin, ready to turn from loving sin to loving the Lord. When John the Baptist was preparing a people to receive the Messiah, they were coming to be baptized because they wanted to have their sins forgiven. To any Jew, preparation for the coming of the Messiah and readiness for His kingdom meant purging the heart of its sinfulness.

You must also enter the narrow gate in utter surrender to Christ. No one can be regenerate, as Christ indicates in Matthew 7, by simply adding Jesus Christ to his carnal activities. Salvation is not an addition; it's a transformation that leads to willing submission to His Word. The whole message of 1 John is that if you are truly redeemed, it will manifest itself in a transformed life in which you confess sin, characteristically obey the Lord, and manifest love for the Lord and others. The divine miracle of a changed life reveals true salvation, resulting in a heart that desires to obey the Lord. As Jesus said, "If you abide in My word, you are My disciples indeed" (John 8:31). . . .

The choice, then, is between these two destinations: the broad way that leads to destruction and the narrow way that is the only highway to heaven. All forms of the religion of human achievement—from humanism and atheism (the ultimate religion of human achievement, where man himself is God) to pseudo-Christianity—are going to end up in the same hell. As John Bunyan said, "For some the entrance to hell is from the portals of heaven." What a shock it's going to be for some people. On the other hand, the narrow way is going to open up into eternal bliss. The broad way narrows down into a terrible pit. The narrow way widens into the endless glories of heaven, the fullness of an unspeakable, everlasting, unclouded fellowship of joy with God that we can't even imagine.

Build Your Life on Him. The broad way that leads to destruction is all sand. The narrow roaders build on rock. What exactly does that mean? We could make a case for the fact that the rock is God, and you are literally building your life on God, which, of course, is true. We could say the rock is God, but so would the Pharisees. Or we could say the rock is Christ. Peter called Him the chief cornerstone (1 Peter 2:6). Paul said He is the Rock (1 Corinthians 10:4).

But plenty of people say they've built their lives on Christ. Most commentators say "rock" in this passage means God or Christ, but I want to take it a step further. Jesus is interested in "whoever hears these sayings of Mine, and does them." The rock is true faith in the Word of God, resulting in an obedient heart and the end of self-righteousness. Yes, God is a rock; yes, Christ is the chief cornerstone. But I believe that what our Lord was saying here is simply this: "These sayings of Mine become the bedrock foundation of the true church, the redeemed church, the true believer."

Look at Matthew 16:13–16: "When Jesus came into the region of Caesarea Philippi, He asked His disciples, saying, 'Who do men say that I, the Son of Man, am?'" And the answer was, "Some say John the Baptist, some Elijah, and others Jeremiah or one of the prophets." But Simon Peter answered, "You are the Christ, the Son of the living God."

Jesus acknowledged this as a revelation, saying, "Flesh and blood has not revealed this to you, but My Father who is in heaven" (verse 17). That is a divine revelation. "And I also say to you that you are Peter"—petros, you are a boulder, a rock—"and on this rock"—petra, bedrock foundation—"I will build My church" (verse 18). And what was the petra, the bedrock of Christianity? It was the Word of God, the Christ, the Son of the living God. The petra of Matthew 16 was the Word of God, and I am convinced that the petra of Matthew 7 is the Word of God as well.

In Acts 20:32, Paul said, "I commend you . . . to the word of His grace, which is able to build you up." It is the Word of God that is our foundation, and it is the Word of God that provides the material for the building as well.

So, our Lord was saying that the person who lives a life in which he only hears and never does is living on the sand of human will, human opinion, human attitudes: the shifting sands of man's self-serving philosophy. Even though you listen, you're not on the rock. On the other hand, the wise man who hears the Word of God and builds his life on God's Word has a rock foundation. His heart has bowed in true faith and submission to the Word of God. And that bears the fruit of obedience.

John 8:30–32: "As He spoke these words, many believed in Him. Then Jesus said to those Jews who believed Him, 'If you abide in My word, you are My disciples indeed. And you shall know the truth, and the truth shall make you free.'" They heard; they truly believed; they accepted; they obeyed. That is building your life on the rock.

In James 1:22, we read this verse: "But be doers of the word, and not hearers only, deceiving yourselves." If you hear Jesus' Sermon on the Mount but don't do it, you're self-deceived; not because I say so, but because the Lord and His disciples say so. First John 2:3: "Now by this we know that we know Him, if we keep His commandments."

When you look at your life, do you see a heart that longs beyond any other desire to obey the Word of God? Or is it disobeying and always justifying that disobedience? Obedience is the key word. The only visible evidence you will ever have of your salvation is a life lived in the direction of obedience; it is the proof that you genuinely have bowed to the lordship of Jesus Christ and been transformed by His grace into a servant of His righteousness.[3]

CONFESSING JESUS AS LORD

To give glory to Christ, we must confess Him as Lord. That's part of salvation, not a subsequent act. Salvation is a matter of confessing that Christ is God and, therefore, that *He* is sovereign in your life.

If you have never confessed Jesus Christ as Lord, you have no capacity to live for His glory. You cannot say, "I deny Christ. He is not my Savior or Lord," and then expect to glorify God. If you dishonor the Son, you dishonor the Father (John 5:23). So salvation is the necessary beginning for glorifying God and, therefore, for spiritual growth. You cannot grow until you are born . . .

When you confessed Jesus as Lord, you did so to the glory of God. Now whatever else you do—even the most mundane functions of life such as eating and drinking—should be focused on the glory of God. That should be the underlying attitude of your life.

Jesus observed His focus in this way: "I honor My Father. . . . I do not seek My own glory" (John 8:49, 50). You will grow spiritually when you follow Christ's example of submitting your life to Christ's lordship; you will be characterized by His humble desire to glorify the Father.[4]

JESUS, YOUR LORD

The phrase "Jesus is Lord" has only three little words, but it's packed with power. Paul wrote to the believers in Corinth: "I want you to understand that no one who is speaking with the help of God's Spirit says, 'Jesus be cursed.' And no one can say, 'Jesus is Lord,' without the help of the Holy Spirit" (1 Corinthians 12:3 NCV). In other words, you can't say that little phrase and mean it with your whole heart unless the Holy Spirit has touched your life and shown you the love of Jesus.

Dr. E. Stanley Jones wasn't very tall, but among evangelists of the twentieth century, this Methodist minister was a giant. He continued to preach into his eighties. Not long before his death in 1973, Jones stood before an audience of college students in Seattle and held up the three middle fingers of his right hand. "Let these fingers call to mind the primary confession of the Christian faith," he said. "Jesus is Lord!"

Obviously those three words provide a way to affirm the fact that Jesus is unlike any other person who has ever lived. But it's also a statement that (when verbalized) unifies those who believe it. Those who recognize Jesus' divinity are drawn together in community. People from different continents, ethnic backgrounds, language groups, and socioeconomic status find common ground by verbalizing that belief.

But unity is not all they find. By admitting that Jesus is the Lord, believers find themselves in a position of acting on what they know. Following are some practical ways we are called to live out our confession of Jesus' identity as Lord.

RESPECT HIM

According to Psalm 111:10, "Wisdom begins with respect for the LORD" (NCV). Respect (also translated "reverence" or "fear") is a healthy understanding of who God is and who we are in relation to him. Because the Jesus who stood up to the angry waves and demanded they calm down is the same One who called the galaxies into existence at the beginning of time, we would do well to act respectfully. Jesus must not be taken for granted.

Yes, Jesus, the Lover of our souls, has given us the privilege to approach him as a Friend, a Teacher, a Healer, a Prince of Peace, a Savior. But that entitlement does not permit us to forget that he is also the Lord of the universe. Too many Christians picture Jesus as a Friend and then treat him poorly. They may consider him as Lover of their souls and then go chasing after other lovers. To have the privilege of a personal relationship with Jesus means friendship with a King. Indeed, that King must continue to be treated with the utmost respect. He's not our peer; he's our Lord.

Show respect for the company you keep.

WORSHIP HIM

Since Jesus is the Lord of the universe, he is entitled to respect. But he deserves more. Respect can be a polite (albeit impersonal) response; even evil dictators and despots are treated with a degree of respect. Along with our respect for Jesus should come a desire to worship him. Because of what he has done for us, we can respond in a deeply personal way. The psalmists wrote:

> *Give unto the LORD the glory due to His name;*
> *Worship the LORD in the beauty of holiness. (Psalm 29:2)*

> *I will worship toward Your holy temple,*
> *And praise Your name*
> *For Your lovingkindness and Your truth;*
> *For You have magnified Your word above all Your name.*
> *(Psalm 138:2)*

Worship involves focusing on the Lord. When we gather with other believers every week, we worship by listening to the preaching of God's Word, singing with heartfelt enthusiasm, and quietly praying during the times set aside for that. We worship when we spend time with the Lord each day—reading his Word, meditating, listening, praying.

We worship when we look into the faces of our children and recognize God's great blessings to us. We worship when we consider the good gifts around us and thank God for them. We worship when we look at a sunset or sunrise and focus on God's wondrous creativity. We worship when we thank him for giving us a beautiful earth on which to live.

We worship when we recognize the lordship of Jesus every day. In the sanctuary of a family room or bedroom at home or a workstation at the office, we can close our eyes and think of Jesus. We worship when we focus on him.

OBEY HIM

Coming to terms with the fact that Jesus is Lord demands more than keeping our distance while giving respect or offering worship.

Lordship implies discipleship. When we recognize there is someone who is the ultimate boss, we also recognize our responsibility
to do what he requests. The defining mark of being a follower of
the Lord is a determination to obey.

Years ago Bob Dylan wrote a song that said it well, entitled
"Gotta Serve Somebody." He made a case for the fact that all
human beings are wired to give themselves fully to some master
and they are obliged to obey whatever master they choose to serve.
For millions, that master is the greed or lust of their sinful souls.
Because Christians acknowledge Jesus as Lord, we are motivated to
serve him and do what he commands.

Obedience to the lordship of Jesus means refusing to rationalize
actions or thoughts that we know he opposes. It means doing the
right thing (even when it's the hard thing). If friends and family
choose another way, we insist on following Jesus' way. An old pastor once advised his congregation, "The key to being a growing
disciple is to be constantly available to the Lord and instantly obedient to what he requests."

How will you know what he requests? You'll know when you
read his Word. As you read a passage of Scripture each day, ask the
Lord to identify an encouragement or truth that should be the
focus of your thinking that day. Underline it, and then refer to it
throughout the day. Over the course of time, as you gather guidance from his Word, you'll instinctively know what he wants you
to do in a variety of situations.

Remember that verse in Psalm 111 that spoke about the importance of respecting the Lord? It also addresses the corresponding
value of obedience. "Wisdom begins with respect for the LORD;
those who obey his orders have good understanding" (verse 10 NCV).

The first-century folks who followed Jesus heard the same
teaching from his lips. The night before Jesus was crucified, he
spoke to his followers about the need for obedience:

Jesus answered and said to him, "If anyone loves Me, he will keep My word; and My Father will love him, and We will come to him and make Our home with him. He who does not love Me does not keep My words; and the word which you hear is not Mine but the Father's who sent Me." (John 14:23–24)

"If you keep My commandments, you will abide in My love, just as I have kept My Father's commandments and abide in His love." (John 15:10)

"You are My friends if you do whatever I command you." (John 15:14)

When we say that Jesus is Lord, we are acknowledging him as our Master who is in charge of our lives. Therefore, we will need to obey him—not only that, we will *want* to obey him. He is a loving Master who wants what is best for us, who wants to give us life in all its fullness (John 10:10).

SHARE HIM

Look around. People everywhere are searching for life that is worthwhile and fulfilling. Since we have discovered that life in Jesus, it makes sense that we would want to tell other people. Based on what we read in the Gospels, Jesus wants us to be one of the means of helping others discovering new life in him. The Lord has given marching orders to give witness to our faith wherever we go (Matthew 28:18–20). And that means much more than simply marking time by hanging with Christians.

Just think of it. If you were a scientist who uncovered a cure for cancer, wouldn't you feel obliged to share your findings with the medical community? Of course you would. Your discovery would save the lives of millions. In much the same way, when our eyes are opened to who Jesus of Nazareth actually is, we can't just nod in agreement as we close our Bibles and return to business as usual. Once we understand that he is the Lord of glory, who has redeemed our world and desires a relationship with every person in it, we need to share the good news!

How many non-Christian people are there in your personal sphere of influence? Who in your family, neighborhood, or work environment doesn't as yet buy into the claims Jesus makes? Those are the individuals the Lord wants you to influence.

Jesus is Lord. The truth about him is found in God's Word, the Bible. Every person must make a decision to either believe in Jesus or not to believe in him.

What's your decision?

SCRIPTURE SELECTIONS

ೞೲ

But why do you call Me "Lord, Lord," and do not do the things which I say?

LUKE 6:46

The word which God sent to the children of Israel, preaching peace through Jesus Christ—He is Lord of all.

ACTS 10:36

And whatever you do in word or deed, do all in the name of the Lord Jesus, giving thanks to God the Father through Him.

COLOSSIANS 3:17

So they said, "Believe on the Lord Jesus Christ, and you will be saved, you and your household."

ACTS 16:31

For the wages of sin is death, but the gift of God is eternal life in Christ Jesus our Lord.

ROMANS 6:23

For if we live, we live to the Lord; and if we die, we die to the Lord. Therefore, whether we live or die, we are the Lord's. For to this end Christ died and rose and lived again, that He might be Lord of both the dead and the living.

ROMANS 14:8–9

You call me Teacher and Lord, and you say well, for so I am.

JOHN 13:13

And He has on His robe and on His thigh a name written:
KING OF KINGS
AND LORD OF LORDS.

REVELATION 19:16

However, Jesus did not permit him, but said to him, "Go home to your friends, and tell them what great things the Lord has done for you, and how He has had compassion on you."

MARK 5:19

He who testifies to these things says, "Surely I am coming quickly." Amen. Even so, come, Lord Jesus!

REVELATION 22:20

Yet for us there is one God, the Father, of whom are all things, and we for Him; and one Lord Jesus Christ, through whom are all things, and through whom we live.

1 CORINTHIANS 8:6

Therefore God also has highly exalted Him and given Him the name which is above every name, that at the name of Jesus every knee should bow, of those in heaven, and of those on earth, and of those under the earth, and that every tongue should confess that Jesus Christ is Lord, to the glory of God the Father.

PHILIPPIANS 2:9–11

That they may know that You, whose name alone is the LORD, Are the Most High over all the earth.

PSALM 83:18

POEMS AND PRAYERS

༄

Lord Jesus, When We Stand Afar

Lord Jesus, when we stand afar
And gaze upon Thy holy cross,
In love of Thee, and scorn of self,
O may we count the world as loss.

When we behold Thy bleeding wounds,
And the rough way that Thou hast trod,
Make us to hate the load of sin
That lay so heavy on our God.

O holy Lord, uplifted high,
With outstretched arms in mortal woe,
Thou dost embrace in wondrous love
The sinful world that lies below.

Give us an ever living faith
To gaze beyond the things we see;
And in the mystery of Thy death
Draw us and all men unto Thee.

—William W. How (1854)

Jesus, I believe that you are the Lord. I believe what you said about yourself and that, as Lord, you have a right to be respected, worshiped, and obeyed. Thank you, Lord, for also being my Savior, Teacher, and Friend. Thank you for being the Mighty Warrior as well as the Prince of Peace. Thank you for loving me; thank you for healing me. Walk with me today and every day, Lord Jesus. Amen.

FOR FURTHER THOUGHT

෩

1. What are some of the opinions you've heard regarding Jesus' identity?
2. How can you put together in your mind the concepts that Jesus is your Friend and yet also your Lord?
3. How can you show more respect for Jesus?
4. In what ways could understanding Jesus as Lord enhance your experience of worship?
5. If you do not believe that Jesus is Lord, what questions do you still have? To whom will you take those questions in order to find the answers?

For further reflection on Jesus as your Lord, listen to "Shout to the Lord" on the companion *Jesus* CD.

Jesus, the Mighty Warrior

FEATURING THE WRITING OF JOHN ELDREDGE

I n a world where some religious extremists terrorize individuals and nations in the name of their god, thinking of Jesus as a Warrior is not a popular concept. However, that reality doesn't make this aspect of Jesus' character any less true.

What was Jesus really like? If you randomly ask people that question, they will likely tell you he was compassionate, understanding, friendly, outgoing, people-loving, and peace-seeking. But is that all he was? While he certainly displayed those characteristics, Jesus is so much more than a meek and mild man. If you have any doubts, consider a few other portraits we see of him in the Gospels. Jesus was, without doubt, quite capable of bold and courageous behavior.

Angered when the temple was used as a marketplace, he was not averse to getting a whip and driving out the moneychangers. Indeed, Jesus was capable of righteous indignation (John 2:15).

When tempted in the wilderness by the evil one, Jesus was not timid or compromising. He refused to be blindsided by Satan's adept twisting of Scripture. Indeed, Jesus gave it right back, using God's Word appropriately of course, until Satan decided it would be better to come back at another time (Luke 4:13).

Jesus didn't mince words for the evil Herod Antipas, a son of Herod the Great who had sought to kill Jesus as a baby by killing every child in Bethlehem (Matthew 2:16). Once when the plotting Pharisees tried to send Jesus into a trap by telling him that Herod was after him, Jesus retorted, "Go, tell that fox . . ." You can be sure that the word "fox" was not a first-century term of endearment.

Jesus also was not tolerant of religious leaders who paraded their piety as a way of gaining attention. His words were not meek and mild as he warned about those who put on a show of religiosity. Jesus told his followers not to be like them. "They have their reward," he said (Matthew 6:2, 5, 16). And their ability to impress others would be the only reward they would ever get.

Even stronger words addressed the issue of legalism. These same pious leaders demanded letter-of-the-law compliance to codes of conduct when such behavior was inhumane. Jesus hated hypocrisy. He detested self-righteousness. "How terrible for you, teachers of the law and Pharisees! You are hypocrites! You close the door for people to enter the kingdom of heaven. You yourselves don't enter, and you stop others who are trying to enter" (Matthew 23:13 NCV). These are not the words of a weakling.

Indeed, it almost seems as if Jesus would purposely heal on the Sabbath even though he knew that those healings would provide ammunition for those who were conspiring against him. He refused to back off. When someone had a need, Jesus met it. He did not defer to the religious sensitivities of those who loved their laws more than the people they were called to serve. Jesus as Lord of the Sabbath would do as he pleased.

Behind the stern face that stared down the Pharisees was the unrelenting countenance of a valiant warrior. Why? Because there's a battle going on. It began in the Garden of Eden and will continue to rage until the end of time. And you and I are right in the thick of it.

John Eldredge reveals the warfare that exists in the spiritual realm and, as a result, affects our lives every single day. We are indeed at war, and we need our Mighty Warrior to fight with us.

READING FROM JOHN ELDREDGE

WE ARE AT WAR

"The thief comes only to steal and kill and destroy; I have come that they may have life, and have it to the full." (John 10:10).

Have you ever wondered why Jesus married those two statements? Did you even know he spoke them at the same time? I mean, he says them in one breath. And he has his reasons. By all means, God intends life for you. But right now that life is opposed. It doesn't just roll in on a tray. There is a thief. He comes to steal and kill and destroy. In other words, yes, the offer is life, but you're going to have to fight for it because there's an Enemy in your life with a different agenda.

There is something set against us.

We are at war.

How I've missed this for so long is a mystery to me. Maybe I've overlooked it; maybe I've chosen not to see. We are at war. I don't like that fact any more than you do, but the sooner we come to terms with it, the better hope we have of making it through to the life we do want. This is not Eden. You probably figured that out. This is not Mayberry; this is not *Seinfeld's* world; this is not *Survivor*. The world in which we live is a combat zone, a violent clash of kingdoms, a bitter struggle unto the death. I'm sorry if I'm the one to break this news to you: you were born into a world at war, and you will live all your days in the midst of a great battle, involving all the forces of heaven and hell and played out here on earth.

Where did you think all this opposition was coming from?

Earlier in the Story, back in the beginning of our time on earth, a great glory was bestowed upon us. We all—men and women—were created in the image of God. Fearfully and wonderfully made, fashioned as living icons of the bravest, wisest, most stunning Person who ever lived. Those who have ever seen him fell to their knees without even thinking about it, as you find yourself breathless before the Grand Canyon or the Alps or the sea at dawn. That glory was shared with us; we were, in Chesterton's phrase, "statues of God walking about in a Garden," endowed with a strength and beauty all our own. All that we ever wished we could be, we were—and more. We were fully alive.

So God created man in his own image, in the image of God he created him; male and female he created them.
(Genesis 1:27 NIV)

When I look at the night sky and see the work of your fingers—
the moon and the stars you have set in place—
what are mortals that you should think of us,
mere humans that you should care for us?
For you made us only a little lower than God,
and you crowned us with glory and honor.
(Psalm 8:3–5 NLT)

I daresay we've heard a bit about original sin, but not nearly enough about original glory, which comes before sin and is deeper to our nature. We were crowned with glory and honor. Why does a woman long to be beautiful? Why does a man hope to be found brave? Because we remember, if only faintly, that we were once more than we are now. The reason you doubt there could be a glory to your life is because that glory has been the object of a long and brutal war.

For lurking in that Garden was an Enemy. This mighty angel had once been glorious as well, the captain of the Lord's hosts, beautiful and powerful beyond compare. But he rebelled against his Creator, led a great battle against the forces of heaven, and was cast down. Banished from his heavenly home, but not destroyed, he waited for an opportunity to take his revenge. Unable to overthrow the Mighty One, he turned his sights on those who bore his image. He lied to us about where true life was to be found, and we believed him. We fell, and "our glory faded," as Milton said, "faded so soon." Or as David lamented, "You turn my glory into shame" (Psalm 4:2).

But God did not abandon us, not by a long shot. I think even a quick read of the Old Testament would be enough to convince you that war is a central theme of God's activity There is the Exodus, where God goes to war to set his captive people free. Blood. Hail. Locusts. Darkness. Death. Plague after plague descends on Egypt like a boxer's one-two punch, like the blows of some great ax. Pharaoh releases his grip, but only for a moment. The fleeing slaves are pinned against the Red Sea when Egypt makes a last charge, hurtling down on them in chariots. God drowns those soldiers in the sea, every last one of them. Standing in shock and joy on the opposite shore, the Hebrews proclaim, "The LORD is a warrior!" (Exodus 15:3). Yahweh is a warrior.

Then it's war to get *to* the promised land. Moses and company have to do battle against the Amalekites; again God comes through, and Moses shouts, "The LORD will be at war against the Amalekites from generation to generation" (Exodus 17:16). Yahweh will be at war. Indeed. You ain't seen nothin' yet. Then it's war to get *into* the promised land—Joshua and the battle of Jericho, all that. After the

Jews gain the promised land, it's war after war to keep it. Israel battles the Canaanites, the Philistines, the Midianites, the Egyptians again, the Babylonians—and on and on it goes. Deborah goes to war; Gideon goes to war; King David goes to war. Elijah wars against the prophets of Baal; Jehoshaphat battles the Edomites. Are you getting the picture?

Many people think the theme of war ends with the Old Testament. Not at all. Jesus says, "I did not come to bring peace, but a sword" (Matthew 10:34). In fact, his birth involved another battle in heaven:

> A great and wondrous sign appeared in heaven: a woman clothed with the sun, with the moon under her feet and a crown of twelve stars on her head. She was pregnant and cried out in pain as she was about to give birth. Then another sign appeared in heaven: an enormous red dragon with seven heads and ten horns and seven crowns on his heads. . . . The dragon stood in front of the woman who was about to give birth, so that he might devour her child the moment it was born. She gave birth to a son, a male child, who will rule all the nations with an iron scepter. . . . And there was war in heaven. Michael and his angels fought against the dragon, and the dragon and his angels fought back. But he was not strong enough, and they lost their place in heaven. . . . Then the dragon was enraged at the woman and went off to make war against the rest of her offspring—those who obey God's commandments and hold to the testimony of Jesus. (Revelation 12:1–5, 7–8, 17)

The birth of Christ was an act of war, an invasion. The Enemy knew it and tried to kill him as a babe (Matthew 2:13). No pale-faced altar boy, the whole life of Christ is marked by battle and confrontation. He kicks out demons with a stern command. He rebukes a fever, and it leaves Peter's mother-in-law. He rebukes a storm, and it subsides. He confronts the Pharisees time and again to set God's people free from legalism. In a loud voice he wakes Lazarus from the dead. He descends to hell, wrestles the keys of hell and death from Satan, and leads a train of captives free (Ephesians 4:8–9; Revelation 1:18). And when he returns, I might point out, Jesus will come mounted on a steed of war, with his robe dipped in blood, armed for battle (Revelation 19:11–15).

War is not just one among many themes in the Bible. It is *the* backdrop for the whole Story, the context for everything else. God is at war. He is trampling out the vineyards where the grapes of wrath are stored. And what is he fighting for? Our freedom and restoration. The glory of God is man fully alive. In the meantime, Paul says, arm yourselves, and the first piece of equipment he urges us to don is the belt of truth (Ephesians 6:10–18). We arm ourselves by getting a good, solid grip on our situation, by getting some clarity on the battle over our lives. God's intentions toward us are life. Those intentions are opposed. Forewarned is fore-armed, as the saying goes. . . .

YOU MUST FIGHT FOR YOUR LIFE

Until we come to terms with *war* as the context of our days we will not understand life. We will misinterpret 90 percent of what is happening around us and to us. It will be very hard to believe that God's intentions toward us are life abundant; it will be even harder not to feel that somehow we are just blowing it. Worse, we will begin to accept some really awful things about God. That four-year-old girl being molested by her daddy—that is "God's *will*"? That ugly divorce that tore your family apart—God wanted that to happen too? And that plane crash that took the lives of so many—that was desired by God?

Most people get stuck at some point because God appears to have abandoned them. He is not coming through. Speaking about her life with a mixture of disappointment and cynicism, a young woman recently said to me, "God is rather silent right now." Yes, it's been awful. I don't discount that for a moment. She is unloved; she is unemployed; she is under a lot. But her attitude strikes me as deeply naive, on the level of someone caught in a cross fire who asks, rather shocked and with a sense of betrayal, "God, why won't you make them stop firing at me?" I'm sorry, but that's not where we are right now. It's not where we are in the Story. That day is coming, *later,* when the lion shall lie down with the lamb and we'll beat swords into plowshares. For now, it's bloody battle.

It sure explains a whole heckuva lot.

Before he promised us life, Jesus warned that a thief would try to steal, kill, and destroy it. How come we don't think that the thief then actually steals, kills, and destroys? You won't understand your life, you won't see clearly what has happened to you or how to live forward from here, unless you see it as battle. A war against your heart. And you are going to need your whole heart for what's coming next. I don't mean what's coming next in the story I'm telling. I mean what's coming next in the life you're living. There are a few things I know, and one thing I do know is this: we don't see things as clearly as we ought to. As we *need* to. We don't understand what's happening around us or to us or to those we love, and we are practically clueless when it comes to the weight of our own lives and the glory that's being . . . held back. . . .

It you're not pursuing a dangerous quest with your life, well, then, you don't need a Guide. If you haven't found yourself in the midst of a ferocious war, then you won't need a seasoned Captain. If you've settled in your mind to live as though this is a fairly neutral world and you are simply trying to live your life as best you can, then you can probably get by with the Christianity of tips and techniques. Maybe. I'll give you about a fifty-fifty chance. But if you intend to live in the Story that God is telling, and if you want the life he offers, then you are going to need more than a handful of principles, however noble they may be. There are too many twists and turns in the road ahead, too many ambushes waiting only God knows where, too much at stake. You cannot possibly prepare yourself for every situation. Narrow is the way, said Jesus. How shall we be sure to find it? We need God intimately, and we need him desperately. . . .

You must fight for your heart

> I will go before you
>> and will level the mountains;
> I will break down gates of bronze
>> and cut through bars of iron.
> I will give you the treasures of darkness,
>> riches stored in secret places,
> so that you may know that I am the Lord,
>> the God of Israel, who summons you by name.
> (Isaiah 45:2–3 NIV)

Doesn't the language of the Bible sometimes sound . . . overblown? Really now—God is going to level mountains for us? We'd be happy if he just helped us get through the week. What's all that about breaking down gates of bronze and cutting through bars of iron? I mean, it sounds heroic, but, well, who's really in need of that? This isn't ancient Samaria. We'd settle for a parking place at the mall. Now, I like the part about treasures of darkness and riches stored in secret places—it reminds me of *Treasure Island* and Long John Silver and all that. What boy hasn't wanted to find buried treasure? And, in fact, those associations make the passage seem like fantasy as well—good poetry, meant to inspire. But not much more.

What if we looked at the passage through the eyes of the heart? That language makes perfect sense if we are living a reality on the mythic level of *Amadeus* or *The Lord of the Rings.* In those stories, gates must be broken down, riches are hidden in darkness, and precious friends must be set free. If we *are* in an epic battle, then the language of the Bible fits perfectly. Things are not what they seem. We are at war. That war is against your heart, your glory. Once more, look at Isaiah 61:1 (NIV):

> He has sent me to bind up the brokenhearted,
>   to proclaim freedom for the captives
>   and release from darkness for the prisoners.

This is God's personal mission for his people; the offer is for us all. So, we must all be held prisoner to some form of darkness. We didn't know it—that's proof enough. In the darkness we can't see. And what is this hidden treasure? Our *hearts*—they are the treasures hidden by darkness. They are not darkness; they are *hidden* by darkness, pinned down, held away in secret places like a hostage held for ransom. Prisoners of war. That is a given. That is assumed. The question is not, *Are* we spiritually oppressed, but *Where* and *How*?

Think of it—why does every story have a villain?

Little Red Riding Hood is attacked by a wolf. Dorothy must face and bring down the Wicked Witch of the West. Qui-Gon Jinn and Obi-Wan Kenobi go hand to hand against Darth Maul. To release the captives of the Matrix, Neo battles the powerful "agents." Frodo is hunted by the Black Riders. (The Morgul blade that the Black Riders pierced Frodo with in the battle on Weathertop—it was aimed at his heart.) Beowulf kills the monster Grendel, and then he has to battle Grendel's mother. Saint George slays the dragon. The children who stumbled into Narnia are called upon by Aslan to battle the White Witch and her armies so that Narnia might be free.

Every story has a villain because *yours* does. You were born into a world at war. When Satan lost the battle against Michael and his angels, "he was hurled to the earth, and his angels with him" (Revelation 12:9 NIV). That means that right now, on this earth, there are hundreds of thousands, if not millions, of fallen angels, foul spirits, bent on our destruction. And what is Satan's mood? "He is filled with fury, because he knows that his time is short" (verse 12 NIV). So what does he spend every day and every night of his sleepless, untiring existence doing? "Then the dragon was enraged at the woman and went off to make war against . . . those who obey God's commandments and hold to the testimony of Jesus" (verse 17 NIV). He has you in his crosshairs, and he isn't smiling.

You have an Enemy. He is trying to steal your freedom, kill your heart, destroy your life. As Satan said through Salieri [in the movie *Amadeus*], "I will hinder and harm Your creature here on earth as far as I am able. I will ruin Your incarnation." Very, very few people live like that. The alarm goes off, and they hit the snooze button, catch a few extra winks, gulp down a cup of coffee on their way to work, wonder why there are so many hassles, grab some lunch, work some more, come home under a sort of cloud, look at the mail, have dinner, watch a little TV, feed the cat, and fall into bed—without once even wondering how the Enemy might be attacking them. All they know is, they sure aren't enjoying that abundant life Christ talked about. . . .

To live in ignorance of spiritual warfare is the most naive and dangerous thing a person can do. It's like skipping through the worst part of town, late at night, waving your wallet above your head. It's like walking into an al-Qaida training camp, wearing an "I love the United States" T-shirt. It's like swimming with great white sharks, dressed as a wounded sea lion and smeared with blood. And let me tell you something: you don't escape spiritual warfare simply because you choose not to believe it exists or because you refuse to fight it.

The bottom line is, you are going to have to fight for your heart. Remember John 10:10—the thief is trying to steal the life God wants to give. . . .

The ministry of Jesus is summarized by one of those who knew him best when Peter brings the gospel to the Gentiles: "God anointed Jesus of Nazareth with the Holy Spirit and power, and . . . he went around doing good and healing all who were under the power of the devil, because God was with him" (Acts 10:38 NIV). In 1 John 3:8, we read, "For this purpose the Son of God was manifested, that He might destroy the works of the devil." The stream of Spiritual Warfare was essential to Jesus' life and ministry. It follows that it must be essential to ours if we would be his followers.[1]

JESUS, YOUR MIGHTY WARRIOR

We were born on a battlefield and a war continues to rage around us. That explains why so much of our lives is sheer drudgery and pain. Knowing that we are engaged in a cosmic conflict helps to explain the heartache and failed expectations that invade what we thought would be the wonderful life we signed up for when we became believers. When the Enemy's attacks come, we wonder how we got onto this battlefield in the first place.

LET JESUS CHANGE YOUR PERSPECTIVE

Having a realistic perspective of the world is the first step in finding confidence on the front lines. We have to start by understanding that we are indeed at war. The reason we so often fail at this very first step is because the Enemy is invisible. We can't hear the mortars falling; we can't see where the Enemy will attack next. The apostle Paul described it this way: "Our fight is not against people on earth but against the rulers and authorities and the powers of this world's darkness, against the spiritual powers of evil in the heavenly world" (Ephesians 6:12 NCV).

"What's all this talk about war?" we might ask. "I didn't enlist," we insist. Ah, but we did. The moment we became Christians, we became Satan's enemies. The battle waging invisibly in the cosmos ended up right over our own heads. There are only two sides—God's or Satan's. We have made our choice, and the devil isn't happy.

So what does Satan do? With his demons doing his bidding, he sets out to make us miserable. Loft a few difficulties our way and make us think God doesn't care. Send a few irresistible temptations and make us think we're failures as believers. Send some legalists along to make us believe we're not really saved because we're not keeping all the right rules. In short, he'll do whatever it might take to make us ineffective and unhappy. And even when we win a decisive victory in a battle, the Enemy doesn't give up. He may retreat for a bit, but he'll be back.

Warrior Jesus doesn't want us to be misled about what we can realistically expect in this life. He told his friends, "In this world you will have trouble" (John 16:33 NIV). Take off those rose-colored glasses. See the world as it is. If the world treated Jesus as an enemy, can we rightly expect any less?

But then Jesus went on. "But take heart! I have overcome the world." The One speaking has a vantage point that allows him to see the end. He knows that the war will not last forever.

Each day, we must enter the battlefield. Fortunately, we do not go into battle alone. Enter Jesus, the Mighty Warrior.

LET JESUS DRESS YOU IN HIS ARMOR

When it comes to suiting up for the front lines of spiritual warfare, our Warrior makes it clear that we need to dress for battle. Here's how the apostle Paul put it:

*Take up the whole armor of God, that you may be able to with-
stand in the evil day, and having done all, to stand. Stand therefore, having girded your waist with truth, having put on the
breastplate of righteousness, and having shod your feet with the
preparation of the gospel of peace; above all, taking the shield of
faith with which you will be able to quench all the fiery darts of
the wicked one. And take the helmet of salvation, and the sword
of the Spirit, which is the word of God. (Ephesians 6:13–17)*

This is serious business. No soldier goes into battle without
armor. Neither should we attempt to live any day of life without the
protection God's armor brings. It doesn't matter whether it feels like
a battle is waging or not; it doesn't matter if we can't hear or see anything at the moment. The battle *is* there, and we must be prepared.

Sure, Jesus was serious when he talked about the promise of
abundant life. Of course life is still full of great joy. Yet every person knows that nothing in this life is perfect; nothing, no matter
how good, lasts forever. The Enemy is still taking aim. The seemingly safe corridors of our office buildings and schools are actually
minefields booby-trapped with potential conflict, disappointment,
relational wounds, and temptations. That's why we need to be
dressed in his armor—today and every day.

Let Jesus put truth around our waist like a belt. This was the
first piece of armor a Roman soldier would put on; it formed the
foundation for the other pieces. Likewise, truth is the foundation
of the Christian life. Knowing we have the truth will help us stand
strong against Satan's lies. Next, Jesus will give us the breastplate of
his righteousness that protects us from Satan's jabs. The shoes will
help us continue to go and tell the message, even in the heat of
battle. We can hold up our shield of faith when Satan sends fiery
darts of doubt, fear, worry, or discouragement. The helmet of sal-

vation protects our minds from doubt. And the sword, the Word of God, helps us fight back. It is our only offensive weapon, and with it we speak God's words back at Satan's lies.

LET JESUS INFUSE YOUR HEART WITH COURAGE

Being dressed in armor is one thing; having the courage to actually go into battle is another. Perhaps we don't think we can do it. Maybe we feel too weak-kneed to be able to do any good at all on the battlefield.

Jesus knows our tendency to turn tail and run. He understands our lack of courage. He knows we've been wounded. He knows when we've been hurt, lost, alone, and frightened. But he's not going to pull us out of the battle—at least not yet. The battlefield is life itself, and we have to cease to be living in order to leave the battle. So if we're alive, we're in the fight, whether we like it or not.

So Jesus gives us armor, but he also gives us courage. In the Old Testament is the story of Joshua, commander of the armies of Israel as they entered the Promised Land. Joshua had a tough act to follow, for he stepped into the shoes of the beloved leader Moses. Listen to God's words to Joshua:

> As I was with Moses, so I will be with you. I will not leave you nor forsake you. Be strong and of good courage. . . . Only be strong and very courageous. . . . Have I not commanded you? Be strong and of good courage; do not be afraid, nor be dismayed, for the LORD your God is with you wherever you go. (Joshua 1:5–9)

Do you think Joshua got the point? In effect God said, "Be strong and be courageous, Joshua. Sure, you have many battles to fight. Giants are in the promised land—that's why the people turned back the last time we were here forty years ago. This is going to be a tough time, but, Joshua, you can have courage because I will not leave you nor forsake you. I will be with you wherever you go."

And what similar words did Jesus give his followers? "Go therefore and make disciples of all the nations, . . . and lo, I am with you
always, even to the end of the age" (Matthew 28:19–20).

Do you get the point? He is with you always. Today, tomorrow,
every day. The battle may be fierce, but he will never leave you nor
forsake you.

LET JESUS DO BATTLE ON YOUR BEHALF

Once we've come to terms with the reality that life is really a war
and that we are combatants in it, we are more prepared to face each
day. But there is another dimension to this warfare that needs to be
considered.

Not only is there a cosmic war around us, there is also a spiritual war within us. We face our signature sins on a daily basis. We
get tripped up by the same temptations over and over. We lose
heart. We lose hope that we'll ever be able to defend ourselves. We
struggle to put our spiritual armor on because the battle raging
within keeps us weakened.

The apostle Paul knew all about this struggle. Listen to his internal battle and see if you can relate:

> *I do not understand the things I do. I do not do what I want to
> do, and I do the things I hate. . . . I want to do the things that
> are good, but I do not do them. I do not do the good things I
> want to do, but I do the bad things I do not want to do. (Romans
> 7:15, 18–19 NCV)*

Not only did Jesus not take us out of the world when we became
believers, he also chose to allow us to battle with sin until the day
we die. So what do we do? Fortunately Paul found the answer to
his dilemma:

What a miserable man I am! Who will save me from this body that brings me death? I thank God for saving me through Jesus Christ our Lord! (Romans 7:24–25 NCV)

Jesus alone is in a position to do battle against the internal enemies you face in the privacy of your heart. Call on Jesus to march into your life and liberate you. Picture the same righteous anger Jesus had toward the moneychangers in the temple as he makes his way into the combat zone of your heart to take out whatever it is that has rendered you a defeated soldier. Jesus, your Mighty Warrior, wants to set you free.

LET JESUS BE YOUR MIGHTY WARRIOR

You may have certain pictures of Jesus hanging in the gallery of your mind. Meek and mild may be one of them—and it is certainly an appropriate picture. It should not be the only one, however. You need to picture Jesus as the coming King of kings, who will one day ride to victory over all evil.

Then I saw heaven opened, and there before me was a white horse. The rider on the horse is called Faithful and True, and he is right when he judges and makes war. His eyes are like burning fire, and on his head are many crowns. . . . Out of the rider's mouth comes a sharp sword that he will use to defeat the nations, and he will rule them with a rod of iron. He will crush out the wine in the winepress of the terrible anger of God the Almighty. On his robe and on his upper leg was written this name: KING OF KINGS AND LORD OF LORDS. (Revelation 19:11–16 NCV)

That is Jesus. He is indeed a Mighty Warrior, not just someday off in the future, but today, on your behalf. A battle is raging and you're right in the middle of it. You need a Mighty Warrior to fight with you.

SCRIPTURE SELECTIONS

୨୦୧

After these things the word of the LORD came to Abram in a vision, saying, "Do not be afraid, Abram. I am your shield, your exceedingly great reward."

GENESIS 15:1

The LORD will fight for you, and you shall hold your peace.

EXODUS 14:14

Happy are you, O Israel!
Who is like you, a people saved by the LORD,
The shield of your help
And the sword of your majesty!
Your enemies shall submit to you,
And you shall tread down their high places.

DEUTERONOMY 33:29

One man of you shall chase a thousand, for the LORD your God is He who fights for you, as He promised you.

JOSHUA 23:10

I will say of the LORD, "He is my refuge and my fortress;
My God, in Him I will trust."

PSALM 91:2

For though we walk in the flesh, we do not war according to the flesh. For the weapons of our warfare are not carnal but mighty in God for pulling down strongholds,

2 CORINTHIANS 10:3–4

These will make war with the Lamb, and the Lamb will over-
come them, for He is Lord of lords and King of kings; and those
who are with Him are called, chosen, and faithful.

Revelation 17:14

The God of my strength, in whom I will trust;
My shield and the horn of my salvation,
My stronghold and my refuge;
My Savior, You save me from violence.

2 Samuel 22:3

Now I saw heaven opened, and behold, a white horse. And He
who sat on him was called Faithful and True, and in righteous-
ness He judges and makes war. His eyes were like a flame of fire,
and on His head were many crowns. He had a name written
that no one knew except Himself.

Revelation 19:11–12

Then David said to the Philistine, "You come to me with a
sword, with a spear, and with a javelin. But I come to you in the
name of the Lord of hosts, the God of the armies of Israel, whom
you have defied. This day the Lord will deliver you into my
hand, and I will strike you and take your head from you. And
this day I will give the carcasses of the camp of the Philistines to
the birds of the air and the wild beasts of the earth, that all the
earth may know that there is a God in Israel."

1 Samuel 17:45–46

POEMS AND PRAYERS

∽

Onward Christian Soldiers

Onward, Christian soldiers, marching as to war,
With the cross of Jesus going on before.
Christ, the royal Master, leads against the foe;
Forward into battle see His banners go!

At the sign of triumph Satan's host doth flee;
On then, Christian soldiers, on to victory!
Hell's foundations quiver at the shout of praise;
Brothers, lift your voices, loud your anthems raise.

Like a mighty army moves the church of God;
Brothers, we are treading where the saints have trod.
We are not divided, all one body we,
One in hope and doctrine, one in charity.

What the saints established that I hold for true.
What the saints believèd, that I believe too.
Long as earth endureth, men the faith will hold,
Kingdoms, nations, empires, in destruction rolled.

Crowns and thrones may perish, kingdoms rise and wane,
But the church of Jesus constant will remain.
Gates of hell can never gainst that church prevail;
We have Christ's own promise, and that cannot fail.

Onward then, ye people, join our happy throng,
Blend with ours your voices in the triumph song.
Glory, laud and honor unto Christ the King,
This through countless ages men and angels sing.

Onward, Christian soldiers, marching as to war,
With the cross of Jesus going on before.

—*Sabine Baring-Gould*

Dear Jesus, thank you that you are a Mighty Warrior. I know sometimes I wonder how I'm going to make it through another day, and then you remind me that you have dressed me in your armor and that you fight alongside me and, at times, *for* me. I am glad that you are strong and mighty—and I'm glad I'm on *your* side!

FOR FURTHER THOUGHT

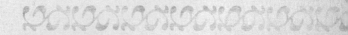

1. How does picturing life as a battlefield give you a different perspective on the problems you face?
2. What "fiery darts" has Satan been shooting at you lately?
3. What piece of armor have you been forgetting to wear (belt of truth, breastplate of righteousness, feet with shoes of the gospel of peace, shield of faith, helmet of salvation, sword of the Spirit—God's Word)?
4. In what situation in your life do you currently need the most courage?
5. What inner battles do you face? How can you let Jesus fight for you?

For further reflection on Jesus as Mighty Warrior, listen to "It's All about Jesus" on the companion *Jesus* CD.

Jesus, the Friend

Someone once observed that we never appreciate our health until we lose it. The same truism can be said of friendship. When we have a quiver full of friends, we often take it for granted and don't recognize how wealthy we are. When relationships break down, friends move away, or someone special dies, we are left with an empty space in our hearts.

Joseph Scriven was a person who felt the pain of loss. He was born into a wealthy Irish family and had the benefit of a prestigious education. A life that appeared blessed soon became riddled with pain, however. The woman he loved more than anything drowned the day before they were to be married. In spite of the support of his family, he felt alone and heartsick.

In an attempt to start over, Joseph moved to Canada where he got a job as a teacher. He used his abilities as an educator to help those in need by tutoring kids. During this time he met another young woman who won his heart. As Joseph began to picture their life together, there is no way he could have imagined the sorrow that would soon frame their romantic bliss. Unbelievably his fiancée fell sick and died before they were married.

Doing his best to resist the pull of despair, Joseph channeled his personal sorrow to identify with the emotional pain of the poor and forgotten. Seeking to live out the principles of the Sermon on the Mount, Joseph gained a reputation of being generous to those in need. His faith in Christ helped him focus on others instead of his own pain.

When he learned that his mother back in Ireland was going through a difficult time, Joseph wrote her a poem. The transparency of his thoughts was based on both his sorrow and his experience of Christ's care, pointing to a friendship with the Savior that he wanted his mother to share.

What a Friend we have in Jesus, all our sins and griefs to bear!
What a privilege to carry everything to God in prayer!
O what peace we often forfeit, O what needless pain we bear,
All because we do not carry everything to God in prayer.

Joseph Scriven, who died in 1888 at the age of sixty-seven, had discovered the importance of a Friend who sticks closer than a brother. Today, more than a century later, the call of the lonely heart still longs for that kind of companionship. In an increasingly depersonalized culture, punctuated by dysfunctional nuclear families and neighborhoods constantly in flux with people moving in and out, it is refreshing to realize that Jesus wants to be your Friend—now and forever. Max Lucado creatively describes Jesus as just such a Friend to those who got to know him best.

READING FROM MAX LUCADO

"As Jesus was going down the road, he saw Matthew sitting at his tax-collection booth. 'Come, be my disciple,' Jesus said to him. So Matthew got up and followed him" (Matt. 9:9 NLT).

The surprise in this invitation is the one invited—a tax collector. Combine the greed of an embezzling executive with the presumption of a hokey television evangelist. Throw in the audacity of an ambulance-chasing lawyer and the cowardice of a drive-by sniper. Stir in a pinch of a pimp's morality, and finish it off with the drug peddler's code of ethics—and what do you have?

A first-century tax collector.

FRIEND OF FLOPS

According to the Jews, these guys ranked barely above plankton on the food chain. Caesar permitted these Jewish citizens to tax almost anything—your boat, the fish you caught, your house, your crops. As long as Caesar got his due, they could keep the rest.

Matthew was a *public* tax collector. Private tax collectors hired other people to do the dirty work. Public publicans, like Matthew, just pulled their stretch limos into the poor side of town and set up shop. As crooked as corkscrews.

His given name was Levi, a priestly name (Mark 2:14; Luke 5:27–28). Did his parents aspire for him to enter the priesthood? If so, he was a flop in the family circle.

You can bet he was shunned. The neighborhood cookouts? Never invited. High-school reunions? Somehow his name was left off the list. The guy was avoided like streptococcus A. Everybody kept his distance from Matthew.

Everyone except Jesus. "'Come, be my disciple,' Jesus said to him. So Matthew got up and followed him" (Matthew 9:9 NLT).

Matthew must have been ripe. Jesus hardly had to tug. Within a punctuation mark, Matthew's shady friends and Jesus' green followers are swapping e-mail addresses. "Then Levi gave a big dinner for Jesus at his house. Many tax collectors and other people were eating there, too" (Luke 5:29 NCV).

What do you suppose led up to that party? Let's try to imagine. I can see Matthew going back to his office and packing up. He removes the Quisling of the Year Award from the wall and boxes up the Shady Business School certificate. His coworkers start asking questions.

"What's up, Matt? Headed on a cruise?"

"Hey, Matthew, the Missus kick you out?"

Matthew doesn't know what to say. He mumbles something about a job change. But as he reaches the door, he pauses. Holding his box full of office supplies, he looks back. They're giving him hangdog looks—kind of sad, puzzled.

He feels a lump in his throat. Oh, these guys aren't much. Parents warn their kids about this sort. Salty language. Mardi Gras morals. They keep the phone number of the bookie on speed dial. The bouncer at the Gentlemen's Club sends them birthday cards. But a friend is a friend. Yet what can he do? Invite them to meet Jesus? Yeah, right. They like preachers the way sheep like butchers. Tell them to tune in to the religious channel on TV? Then they'd think cotton-candy hair is a requirement for following Christ. What if he snuck little Torah tracts in their desks? Nah, they don't read.

So, not knowing what else to do, he shrugs his shoulders and gives them a nod. "These stupid allergies," he says, rubbing the mist from one eye.

Later that day the same thing happens. He goes to the bar to settle up his account. The décor is blue-collar chic: a seedy, smoky place with a Budweiser chandelier over the pool table and a jukebox in the corner. Not the country club, but for Matthew, it's his home on the way home. And when he tells the owner he's moving on, the bartender responds, "Whoa, Matt. What's comin' down?"

Matthew mumbles an excuse about a transfer but leaves with an empty feeling in his gut.

Later on he meets up with Jesus at a diner and shares his problem. "It's my buddies—you know, the guys at the office. And the fellows at the bar."

"What about them?" Jesus asks.

"Well, we kinda run together, you know. I'm gonna miss 'em. Take Josh for instance—as slick as a can of Quaker State, but he visits orphans on Sunday. And Bruno at the gym? Can crunch you like a roach, but I've never had a better friend. He's posted bail for me three times."

Jesus motions for him to go on. "What's the problem?"

"Well, I'm gonna miss those guys. I mean, I've got nothing against Peter and James and John, Jesus . . . but they're Sunday morning, and I'm Saturday night. I've got my own circle, ya know?"

Jesus starts to smile and shake his head. "Matthew, Matthew, you think I came to quarantine you? Following me doesn't mean forgetting your friends. Just the opposite. I want to meet them."

"Are you serious?"

"Is the high priest a Jew?"

"But, Jesus, these guys . . . half of them are on parole. Josh hasn't worn socks since his Bar Mitzvah . . ."

"I'm not talking about a religious service, Matthew. Let me ask you—what do you like to do? Bowl? Play Monopoly? How's your golf game?"

Matthew's eyes brighten. "You ought to see me cook. I get on steaks like a whale on Jonah."

"Perfect." Jesus smiles. "Then throw a little going-away party. A hang-up-the-clipboard bash. Get the gang together."

Matthew's all over it. Calling the caterer, his housekeeper, his secretary. "Get the word out, Thelma. Drinks and dinner at my house tonight. Tell the guys to come and bring a date."

And so Jesus ends up at Matthew's house, a classy split-level with a view of the Sea of Galilee. Parked out front is everything from BMWs to Harleys to limos. And the crowd inside tells you this is anything but a clergy conference.

Earrings on the guys and tattoos on the girls. Moussified hair. Music that rumbles teeth roots. And buzzing around in the middle of the group is Matthew, making more connections than an electrician. He hooks up Peter with the tax collector bass club and Martha with the kitchen staff. Simon the Zealot meets a high-school debate partner. And Jesus? Beaming. What could be better? Sinners and saints in the same room, and no one's trying to determine who is which. But an hour or so into the evening the door opens, and an icy breeze blows in. "The Pharisees and the men who taught the law for the Pharisees began to complain to Jesus' followers, 'Why do you eat and drink with tax collectors and sinners?'" (Luke 5:30 NCV).

Enter the religious police and their thin-lipped piety. Big black books under arms. Cheerful as Siberian prison guards. Clerical collars so tight that veins bulge. They like to grill too. But not steaks.

Matthew is the first to feel the heat. "Some religious fellow you are," one says, practically pulling an eyebrow muscle. "Look at the people you hang out with."

Matthew doesn't know whether to get mad or get out. Before he has time to choose, Jesus intervenes, explaining that Matthew is right where he needs to be. "Healthy people don't need a doctor—sick people do. I have come to call sinners to turn from their sins, not to spend my time with those who think they are already good enough" (verses 31–32 NLT).

Quite a story. Matthew goes from double-dealer to disciple. He throws a party that makes the religious right uptight, but Christ proud. The good guys look good, and the bad guys hit the road. Some story indeed.

What do we do with it?

That depends on which side of the tax collector's table you find yourself. You and I are Matthew. Don't look at me that way. There's enough hustler in the best of us to qualify for Matthew's table. Maybe you've never taken taxes, but you've taken liberty with the truth, taken credit that wasn't yours, taken advantage of the weak. You and me? Matthew.

If you're still at the table, you receive an invitation. "Follow me." So what if you've got a rube reputation? So did Matthew. You may end up writing your own gospel.

If you've left the table, you receive a clarification. You don't have to be weird to follow Jesus. You don't have to stop liking your friends to follow him. Just the opposite. A few introductions would be nice. Do you know how to grill a steak?

Sometime ago I was asked to play a game of golf. The foursome included two preachers, a church leader, and a "Matthew, B.C." The thought of four hours with three Christians, two of whom were pulpiteers, did not appeal to him. His best friend, a Christ follower and his boss, insisted, so he agreed. I'm happy to report that he proclaimed the experience painless. On the ninth hole he turned to one of us and said, smiling, "I'm so glad you guys are normal." I think he meant this: "I'm glad you didn't get in my face or club me with a King James driver. Thanks for laughing at my jokes and telling a few yourself. Thanks for being normal." We didn't lower standards. But neither did we saddle a high horse. We were nice. Normal and nice.

Discipleship is sometimes defined by being normal.

A woman in a small Arkansas community was a single mom with a frail baby. Her neighbor would stop by every few days and keep the child so she could shop. After some weeks her neighbor shared more than time; she shared her faith, and the woman did what Matthew did. She followed Christ.

The friends of the young mother objected. "Do you know what those people teach?" they contested.

"Here is what I know," she told them. "They held my baby."

I think Jesus likes that kind of answer, don't you?

FRIEND OF THE DISCOURAGED

There is a look that says, "It's too late." You've seen it. The rolling of the eyes, the shaking of the head, the pursing of the lips.

Your friend is a day from divorce. Over coffee you urge, "Can't you try one more time?"

She shrugs. "Done that."

Your father and brother don't speak to one another. Haven't for years. "Won't you try again?" you ask your dad. He looks away, inhales deeply, and sighs.

Five years this side of retirement the economy Hindenburgs your husband's retirement. You try to make the best of it. "You can go back to school. Learn a new trade." You might as well have told him to swim to London. He shakes his head. "I'm too old . . . It's too late."

Too late to save a marriage.

Too late to reconcile.

Too late for a new career.

Too late to catch any fish. Or so Peter thinks. All night he fished. He witnessed both the setting and the rising of the sun but has nothing to show for it. While other fishermen cleaned their catch, he just cleaned his nets. But now Jesus wants him to try again.

"Now it happened that while the crowd was pressing around Him and listening to the word of God, [Jesus] was standing by the lake of Gennesaret" (Luke 5:1 NASBU).

The Sea of Gennesaret, or Galilee, is a six-by-thirteen-mile body of water in northern Israel. These days her shore sleeps, attracting only a cluster of tour buses and a handful of fishermen. But in the days of Jesus the area bustled with people. Nine of the seacoast villages boasted populations of fifteen thousand plus. And you get the impression that a good portion of those people was present the morning Christ ministered on the beach. As more people arrived, more people pressed. With every press, Jesus took a step back. Soon he was stepping off the sand and into the water. That's when he had an idea.

> He saw two boats lying at the edge of the lake; but the fishermen had gotten out of them and were washing their nets. And He got into one of the boats, which was Simon's, and asked him to put out a little way from the land. And He sat down and began teaching the people from the boat. When He had finished speaking, He said to Simon, "Put out into the deep water and let down your nets for a catch." (verses 2–4 NASBU)

Jesus needs a boat; Peter provides one. Jesus preaches; Peter is content to listen. Jesus suggests a midmorning fishing trip, however, and Peter gives him a look. The it's-too-late look. He runs his fingers through his hair and sighs, "Master, we worked hard all night and caught nothing" (verse 5 NASBU). Can you feel Peter's futility?

All night the boat floated fishless on the black sheet of the sea. Lanterns of distant vessels bounced like fireflies. The men swung their nets and filled the air with the percussion of their trade.

Swish, slap . . . silence.

Swish, slap . . . silence.

Midnight.

Excited voices from across the lake reached the men. Another boat had found a school. Peter considered moving but decided against it.

Swish, slap . . . silence.

Two o'clock in the morning. Peter rested while his brother fished. Then Andrew rested. James, floating nearby, suggested a move. The others agreed. Wind billowed the sails and blew the boats to a cove. The rhythm resumed.

Swish, slap . . . silence.

Every yank of the net was easy. Too easy. This night the lake was a proper lady. No matter how often the men winked and whistled, she offered nothing.

Golden shafts eventually reclaimed the sky. Most mornings the sunrise inspires the men. Today it only tired them. They didn't want to see it. Who wants to dock an empty boat? Who wants to tie up and clean up, knowing the first question the wife is going to ask? And, most of all, who wants to hear a well-rested carpenter-turned-rabbi say, "Put out into the deep water and let down your nets for a catch" (verse 4 NASBU)?

Oh, the thoughts Peter might have had. *I'm tired. Bone tired. I want a meal and a bed, not a fishing trip. Am I his tour guide? Besides, half of Galilee is watching. I feel like a loser already. Now he wants to put on a midmorning fishing exhibition? You can't catch fish in the morning. Count me out.*

Whatever thoughts Peter had were distilled to one phrase: "We worked hard all night and caught nothing" (verse 5 NASBU).

Do you have any worn, wet, empty nets? Do you know the feeling of a sleepless, fishless night? Of course you do. For what have you been casting?

Sobriety? "I've worked so hard to stay sober, but . . ."

Solvency? "My debt is an anvil around my neck . . ."

Faith? "I want to believe, but . . ."

Healing? "I've been sick so long . . ."

A happy marriage? "No matter what I do . . ."

I've worked hard all night and caught nothing.

You've felt what Peter felt. You've sat where Peter sat. And now

Jesus is asking you to go fishing. He knows your nets are empty. He knows your heart is weary. He knows you'd like nothing more than to turn your back on the mess and call it a life.

But he urges, "It's not too late to try again."

See if Peter's reply won't help you formulate your own. "I will do as You say and let down the nets" (verse 5 NASBU).

Not much passion in those words. You might hope for a ten-thousand-candle smile and a fist pumping the air. "I got Jesus in my boat. Momma, warm up the oven!" But Peter shows no excitement. He feels none. Now he has to unfold the nets, pull out the oars, and convince James and John to postpone their rest. He has to work. If faith is measured in seeds, his is an angstrom. Inspired? No. But obedient? Admirably. And an angstrom of obedience is all Jesus wants.

"Put out into the deep water," the God-man instructs.

Why the deep water? You suppose Jesus knew something Peter didn't? You suppose Jesus is doing with Peter what we parents do with our kids on Easter Sunday? They find most of the eggs on their own. But a couple of treasures inevitably survive the first harvest. "Look," I'd whisper in the ears of my daughters, "behind the tree." A quick search around the trunk, and, what do you know, Dad was right. Spotting treasures is easy for the one who hid them. Finding fish is simple for the God who made them. To Jesus, the Sea of Galilee is a dollar-store fishbowl on a kitchen cabinet.

Peter gives the net a swish, lets it slap, and watches it disappear. Luke doesn't tell us what Peter did while he was waiting for the net to sink, so I will. (I'm glancing heavenward for lightning.)

I like to think that Peter, while holding the net, looks over his shoulder at Jesus. And I like to think that Jesus, knowing Peter is about to be half yanked into the water, starts to smile. A daddy-daughter-Easter-egg smile. Rising cheeks render his eyes

half-moons. A dash of white flashes beneath his whiskers. Jesus
tries to hold it back but can't.

There is so much to smile about. It's Easter Sunday, and the
lawn is crawling with kids. Just wait till they look under the tree.

> *When they had done this, they enclosed a great quantity of
> fish, and their nets began to break; so they signaled to their
> partners in the other boat for them to come and help them.
> And they came and filled both of the boats, so that they
> began to sink. (verses 6–7 NASBU)*

Peter's arm is yanked into the water. It's all he can do to hang
on until the other guys can help. Within moments the four fishermen and the carpenter are up to their knees in flopping silver.

Peter lifts his eyes off the catch and onto the face of Christ. In
that moment, for the first time, he sees Jesus. Not Jesus the Fish
Finder. Not Jesus the Multitude Magnet. Not Jesus the Rabbi. Peter
sees Jesus the Lord.

Peter falls face first among the fish. Their stink doesn't bother
him. It is his stink that he's worried about. "Go away from me
Lord, for I am a sinful man!" (verse 8 NASBU).

Christ had no intention of honoring that request. He doesn't
abandon self-confessed schlemiels. Quite the contrary, he enlists them.
"Do not fear, from now on you will be catching men" (verse 10 NASBU).

Contrary to what you may have been told, Jesus doesn't limit his
recruiting to the stout-hearted. The beat up and worn out are prime
prospects in his book, and he's been known to climb into boats,
bars, and brothels to tell them, "It's not too late to start over."

Peter learned the lesson. But wouldn't you know it? Peter for-
got the lesson. Two short years later this man who confessed
Christ in the boat cursed Christ at a fire. The night before Jesus'
crucifixion, Peter told people that he'd never heard of Jesus.

He couldn't have made a more tragic mistake. He knew it. The burly fisherman buried his bearded face in thick hands and spent Friday night in tears. All the feelings of that Galilean morning came back to him.

It's too late.

But then Sunday came. Jesus came! Peter saw him. Peter was convinced that Christ had come back from the dead. But apparently Peter wasn't convinced that Christ came back for him.

So he went back to the boat—to the same boat, the same beach, the same sea. He came out of retirement. He and his buddies washed the barnacles off the hull, unpacked the nets, and pushed out. They fished all night, and, honest to Pete, they caught nothing.

Poor Peter. Blew it as a disciple. Now he's blowing it as a fisherman. About the time he wonders if it's too late to take up carpentry, the sky turns orange, and they hear a voice from the coastline. "Had any luck?"

They yell back, "No."

"Try the right side of the boat!"

With nothing to lose and no more pride to protect, they give it a go. "So they cast, and then they were not able to haul it in because of the great number of fish" (John 21:6 NASBU). It takes a moment for the déjà vu to hit Peter. But when it does, he cannonballs into the water and swims as fast as he can to see the one who loved him enough to *re-create* a miracle. This time the message stuck.

Peter never again fished for fish. He spent the rest of his days telling anyone who would listen, "It's not too late to try again."

Is it too late for you? Before you say yes, before you fold up the nets and head for the house—two questions. Have you given Christ your boat? Your heartache? Your dead-end dilemma? Your struggle? Have you really turned it over to him? And have you gone deep? Have you bypassed the surface-water solutions you can see in search of the deep-channel provisions God can give? Try the other side of the boat. Go deeper than you've gone. You may find what Peter found. The payload of his second effort was not the fish he caught but the God he saw.

The God-man who spots weary fishermen, who cares enough to enter their boats, who will turn his back on the adoration of a crowd to solve the frustration of a friend. The next door Savior who whispers this word to the owners of empty nets, "Let's try again—this time with me on board."[1]

JESUS, YOUR FRIEND

Some Christians think of God as judgmental, aloof, and unapproachable. The Bible, however, gives a different picture. Jesus was God in human form. While the Gospel narratives indeed show us a man of serious determination (who whipped moneychangers out of the temple, held his own against the ultralegalistic religious leaders, and marched resolutely to his own death), they also reveal a man of humor and compassion. He stooped to hold children. He told great stories. He sought out the lonely and disenfranchised, such as when he looked up into a tree and called down Zacchaeus, a not-so-well-liked tax collector, to have dinner with him. Jesus went to a wedding and miraculously made new wine for the celebration. He visited Matthew's home and ate dinner with the "undesirables," earning him the label "friend of tax collectors and sinners" (Matthew 11:19). As noted in the reading above, he twice provided the same miracle for his dear friend Peter, just to help him understand who he was and what he could do.

Jesus left his exalted place in heaven to pitch his tent on our imperfect planet. His great love for us was his motivation to put on our skin in order to take on our sin. He died so that we could have a personal relationship with him—so we could be his *friends*. "Greater love has no one than this, than to lay down one's life for his friends," Jesus said (John 15:13). Even though we no longer see him with our physical eyes, Jesus our Friend continues to reach out to us, a big smile on his lips at the joy he wants to bring us.

Like any good friend, Jesus knows us at our best as well as at our worst—and loves us anyway. In spite of the fact that he knows we'll disappoint him (as happens even between the best of friends), he will always forgive and always be there for us. He came not to condemn, but to save. As Jesus told the probing Pharisee Nicodemus: "For God so loved the world that He gave His only begotten Son, that whoever believes in Him should not perish but have everlasting life. For God did not send His Son into the world to condemn the world, but that the world through Him might be saved" (John 3:16–17). Those are the words of One who is affirming his desire to befriend us, to love us, to save us, to forgive us.

Jesus takes the initiative to be our Friend. But friendship goes two ways. The depth of our friendship with Jesus depends on our willingness to *be his friend* in return.

WALK WITH HIM

Friends walk together. The prophet Amos understood this when he asked the question, "Can two walk together, unless they are agreed?" (Amos 3:3). In order to have a spiritual friendship with Jesus, we need to "walk" with him—to consciously and purposefully bring his loving presence into our daily life. That means wherever we go, he goes. Whatever conversations we have, he's right there listening. This perspective on an intimate friendship with Jesus can be sobering. We might look at our daily routines differently when we think about bringing our best Friend along with us. Are what we are doing, the places we are going, and the topics we are discussing pleasing to him? Are we in agreement with Christ, as Amos observed, so we can walk together as friends?

This idea may be new to you. Walking with Jesus may cause you to make some needed changes. Jesus is not along to be a kill-joy to ruin your fun or an intrusive paparazzi hoping to find a way to embarrass you. Instead, he wants to be your Friend, to be a part of everything you do, to infuse your life with joy and richness. He says, "I came to give life—life in all its fullness" (John 10:10 NCV). Those are friendship words. This Friend who sticks closer than a brother wants to enrich your life with his presence. He wants to share your experiences with you. When was the last time you took a moment to simply acknowledge Jesus' presence in every moment of your life?

SPEND TIME WITH HIM

Like anything else worth having, friendship requires maintenance. Individuals who value a shared bond make time to be together. Shared experiences are the stuff of which growing friendships are made. Enjoying a relationship with the Lord is no different. We need to set aside time to spend with our best Friend.

In his little booklet, "My Heart Christ's Home," Robert Boyd Munger pictures Jesus as a houseguest who comes to visit the "home" of a new believer. As Jesus tours each room of the Christian's heart, the homeowner is challenged to make changes in furnishings and activities in light of this Guest's presence. Then Jesus takes up residence, as he has been asked to do. Every morning he patiently waits for the Christian to come and spend a few moments in quiet conversation. For a while, this occurs on a regular basis. But soon the Christian gets busy and the appointments are forgotten, missed, or simply seen as a nuisance. A poignant portion of the story finds Jesus waiting as usual to spend time with the Christian. But the Christian is once again too busy, on the way to this or that. So Jesus sits on the couch and waits.

Not a good way to treat any friend. Not a good way to treat the best Friend.

Jesus wants to spend time with you. While overly-structured quiet times can quickly become stale and stiff, scheduling and keeping regular appointments with the Lord are essential. Friends find time for each other and don't allow competing conflicts to get in the way. After all, you probably have issues that you need to bring up with him. And guess what? He has concerns (spelled out in his Word) that he wants to bring to your attention as well. So schedule time with your best Friend every day—put it right on your calendar like any other important appointment. Don't miss the opportunity to spend time with your best Friend.

CONVERSE WITH HIM

Close friends communicate with each other. If they live near each other, that verbal exchange is in person. If miles separate such friends, they still make the effort to somehow stay in touch. Our relationship with Jesus also will grow as we spend time conversing with him.

That conversation takes the form of prayer—both the on-our-knees kind of prayers and the prayers breathed all day long as part of our daily routine. It can be as formal as saying the Lord's Prayer before our family dinner, or as informal as calling out for his help and guidance when we're lost, driving in an unfamiliar city. We can pray by listening to music that soothes our souls and helps us focus on the greatness of God. Prayer even includes those times we are speechless, when we can't find words to express intense sadness or great joy. (Remember, friends don't always need words to identify with what the other person is feeling.)

Conversing with Jesus is not just talking *at* him, however. Prayer, as a conversation with any friend, is not a monologue; it's always dialogue. Jesus wants to express himself to us. He speaks through his Word, the Bible. He also whispers in our hearts— usually not with audible words, but through impressions and promptings that are easily detected when we quiet our hearts, ask questions, and listen. Because Jesus is alive and present in our world, it should come as no surprise that this Friend not only desires to speak to us, but does indeed speak when we are quietly listening.

Do you consider Jesus to be your Friend? Then talk to him!

WRITE TO HIM

Sound a bit odd? Writing out our feelings and thoughts is often referred to as journaling. That's what is meant here—writing letters to Jesus that only you will ever see.

For some, journaling comes as naturally as breathing; some people would much rather write their feelings than try to express them verbally. Writing down one's thoughts and prayers can provide an intimate opportunity to examine your relationship with Christ, to keep a record of events, prayer requests, and concerns, as well as to record the joy of prayers answered and guidance received. The Bible is proof of how deeply words preserved on paper can speak to a person's heart. Like a love letter, you can read and reread a deeply personal passage over and over. And because of the power of the written word, what you have to say to the Lord can be effectively expressed that way as well.

Jesus wants to be your Friend. He wants you to understand your relationship with him not as a servant to a Master, but as a friend to a Friend. At the Last Supper, Jesus told his disciples, "I no longer call you servants, because a servant does not know what his master is doing. But I call you friends, because I have made known to you everything I heard from my Father" (John 15:15 NCV).

What a Friend we have in Jesus!

Scripture Selections

∞

So the LORD spoke to Moses face to face, as a man speaks to his friend. And he would return to the camp, but his servant Joshua the son of Nun, a young man, did not depart from the tabernacle.

EXODUS 33:11

A friend loves at all times,
And a brother is born for adversity.

PROVERBS 17:17

A man who has friends must himself be friendly,
But there is a friend who sticks closer than a brother.

PROVERBS 18:24

Faithful are the wounds of a friend,
But the kisses of an enemy are deceitful.

PROVERBS 27:6

"Go therefore and make disciples of all the nations, baptizing them in the name of the Father and of the Son and of the Holy Spirit, teaching them to observe all things that I have commanded you; and lo, I am with you always, even to the end of the age." Amen.

MATTHEW 28:19–20

And Jesus said to them, "Can the friends of the bridegroom fast while the bridegroom is with them? As long as they have the bridegroom with them they cannot fast."

MARK 2:19

The Son of Man has come eating and drinking, and you say, "Look, a glutton and a winebibber, a friend of tax collectors and sinners!"

LUKE 7:34

Greater love has no one than this, than to lay down one's life for his friends. You are My friends if you do whatever I command you. No longer do I call you servants, for a servant does not know what his master is doing; but I have called you friends, for all things that I heard from My Father I have made known to you.

JOHN 15:13–15

And the Scripture was fulfilled which says, "Abraham believed God, and it was accounted to him for righteousness." And he was called the friend of God.

JAMES 2:23

Adulterers and adulteresses! Do you not know that friendship with the world is enmity with God? Whoever therefore wants to be a friend of the world makes himself an enemy of God.

JAMES 4:4

POEMS AND PRAYERS

ᗧᗣ

What a Friend We Have in Jesus

What a Friend we have in Jesus, all our sins and griefs to bear!
What a privilege to carry everything to God in prayer!
O what peace we often forfeit, O what needless pain we bear,
All because we do not carry everything to God in prayer.

Have we trials and temptations? Is there trouble anywhere?
We should never be discouraged; take it to the Lord in prayer.
Can we find a friend so faithful who will all our sorrows share?
Jesus knows our every weakness; take it to the Lord in prayer.

Are we weak and heavy laden, cumbered with a load of care?
Precious Savior, still our refuge, take it to the Lord in prayer.
Do your friends despise, forsake you? Take it to the Lord in prayer!
In His arms He'll take and shield you; you will find a solace there.

Blessed Savior, Thou hast promised Thou wilt all our burdens bear.
May we ever, Lord, be bringing all to Thee in earnest prayer.
Soon in glory bright unclouded there will be no need for prayer,
Rapture, praise and endless worship will be our sweet portion there.

—Joseph M. Scriven

Dear Jesus, thank you for wanting to be my Friend. Thank you that you will never let me down and will always be there for me, tell me the truth when I need to hear it, comfort me when I'm hurting, and rejoice with me when I rejoice. Help me to be your friend as well. Help me to remember to walk with you every day, to talk with you, and to spend time with you. Thanks for dying on the cross so that you and I could be friends. Amen.

FOR FURTHER THOUGHT

1. How would you describe your relationship with Jesus? Is "friendship" a word that comes to mind?
2. Do you walk through each day with Jesus? What changes might need to take place in your daily routine if you picture Jesus with you at all times?
3. Do you have a regular quiet time with Jesus? If not, when can you put that into your schedule?
4. What types of conversation do you have with Jesus? How can you make it more natural to converse with him throughout your day?
5. How might you include journaling in your spiritual growth?

For further reflection on Jesus as your Friend, listen to "All To Thee" on the companion *Jesus* CD.

Jesus, the Teacher

FEATURING THE WRITING OF CHARLES SWINDOLL

Everyone has a favorite teacher. For some, it was that elementary teacher who patiently helped them as they struggled with reading until, one day, the words on the page made sense. For others, it might be that high-school geometry teacher who explained the theorems over and over, and even stayed after school a few times to give extra help until they finally "got it." Maybe some people will think of a Sunday school teacher who brought the Bible stories to life. Others might fondly recall the teacher who saw something special in them—a spark of creative expression or an ability to organize facts—and encouraged and nurtured that gift.

Memorable teachers come in all shapes and sizes, but one thing they have in common is the ability to communicate facts in a fun and creative way. They have a knack for simplifying the complex and elevating the mundane. They are passionate about the subject matter they convey. Memorable teachers take an interest in their students. They motivate them both inside and outside the classroom. They are approachable. They are committed to helping those under their tutelage succeed. They go the extra mile.

So, who is the most memorable teacher in your life? Why do you remember that person so fondly?

Like that teacher who left his or her imprint on your life, Jesus was a Teacher who made an impact on the lives of his students. The Gospels reveal him to be creative, innovative, even humorous. No blackboard and chalk were necessary, although he would use his finger to write in the chalklike dirt if needed.

Jesus was intentional in the way he communicated. He knew how to punctuate his lessons in ways that helped his learners learn. He who was the "Logos of God" packaged the truth of eternity in ordinary wrapping that common fishermen and day laborers could unpack. Creating his own curriculum, he used visual aids like fish and bread. He told stories about farmers and travelers and thieves. He used drama, walking on the water or stilling the storm. He not only spoke in an idiom his disciples understood, he used word pictures to punctuate his principles. And to prove that his words were true, he performed miracles.

Jesus was approachable, not aloof. He modeled integrity. He willingly "stayed after" and explained the meaning of a parable if his disciples didn't get it. The lessons that fell from his lips were lived out in his life. The kingdom of God was not just a subject matter to be mastered; it was a lifestyle to be lived. To that end, he challenged his followers with questions that demanded thought and response. By observing their interactions with one another, with their critics, and with the masses, he quizzed them on their comprehension. Committed to their success, he awakened within them a desire to know more.

Teacher of the Year? More like Teacher of the Ages! Charles Swindoll offers some insights into Jesus as the master Teacher.

Reading from Charles Swindoll

When it came to clear communication, Jesus was a master. Children and adults alike had no difficulty understanding His words or following His reasoning. This is remarkable because while He was on earth He lived in a society that had become accustomed to cliché-ridden religious double-talk. The scribes, priests, and Pharisees who dominated the synagogue scene in Palestine saw to that. They unintentionally made Jesus' simple style and straightforward approach seem all the more refreshing. When He spoke, people listened. Unlike the pious professionals of His day, Jesus' words made sense.

This was never truer than when He sat down on a hillside with a group of His followers and talked about what really mattered. Thanks to tradition, this teaching session has come to be known as the Sermon on the Mount—in my opinion, an unfortunate title. His words were authoritative but not officious, insightful but not sermonic. His hillside chat was an informal, reasonable, thoughtful, and unpretentious presentation. He distilled an enormous amount of truth in an incredibly brief period of time, and those who had endured a lifetime of boring and irrelevant sermons sat spellbound to the end.

The result was that when Jesus had finished these words, the multitudes were amazed at His teaching; for He was teaching them as one having authority, and not as their scribes. (Matthew 7:28–29 NASB)

If we fail to understand the background behind that statement, we will not appreciate the depth of His listeners' gratitude. In short, they were fed up with the manipulation, the pride, and especially the hypocrisy of their religious leaders. Long years of legalism, mixed with the pharisaic power plays designed to intimidate and control, held the general public in bondage. Man-made systems of complicated requirements and backbreaking demands shut the people behind invisible bars, shackled in chains of guilt. They could not measure up; they could not quite keep their heads above water unless they dog-paddled like mad . . . and many were losing heart. But who dared say so?

Out of the blue came Jesus with His message of liberating grace, encouragement to the weary, hope for the sinful. Best of all, every-thing He said was based on pristine truth—God's truth—instead of rigid religious regulations. He talked of faith—simple faith—in terms anyone could understand. His "yes face" invited them in as His teaching released them from guilt and shame, fear and confu-sion. The Nazarene's authenticity caught them off guard, disarmed their suspicions, and blew away the fog that had surrounded organized religion for decades. No wonder the people found Him amazing! No wonder the grace-killing scribes and Pharisees found Him unbearable! Hypocrisy despises authenticity. When truth unmasks wrong, those who are exposed get very nervous. . . .

The boldness of authenticity is beautiful to behold, unless, of course, you happen to be a hypocrite. That explains why Jesus' words, which brought such comfort to those who followed Him, enraged the Pharisees. Although He never called one of them by name during His hillside talk, He exposed their legalistic lifestyle as no one had ever done before. Count on it: They knew what He was saying.

On the surface, Jesus' words, recorded in Matthew 5, 6, and 7, may seem calm in tone and basic in their simplicity. We can read them in fifteen or twenty minutes, and at first glance they appear to be nothing more than a gentle tap on the shoulder. But to those who had twisted religion into a performance-oriented list of demands and expectations, they were nothing short of a bold exposé.

When Moses came down from Mount Sinai centuries earlier, he did not bring Ten Suggestions; likewise, when Jesus delivered His message from the mount, it was no humble homily. To legalists His words represented a howling reproach that continues into the modern age. Jesus' words may be simple, but they are definitely not insipid.

JESUS' WORDS: A PLEA FOR TRUE RIGHTEOUSNESS

Behind Jesus' teaching on the Palestinian hillside was a deep concern for those who had surrendered their lives to the tyranny of pressure that was light-years away from simple faith. Of special concern to Him was the possibility that some had gotten sucked into the pharisaic model of substituting the artificial for the authentic, a danger that always lurks in the shadows of legalism.

That is what leads me to believe that the major message of Jesus' teaching in this setting could be encapsulated in these five words He spoke: "Do not be like them" (Matthew 6:8 NASB).

Our Lord wants His true followers to be distinct, unlike the majority who follow the herd. In solving conflicts, doing business, and responding to difficulties, Jesus' people are not to maintain the same attitudes or choose the priorities of the majority. And for sure, we are not to emulate pharisaism. When Jesus teaches, "Do not be like them," He really means it. Hypocrisy, He hates . . . authenticity, He loves.

Hypocrisy permits us to travel both sides of the path—to look righteous but be unholy, to sound pious but be secretly profane. Invariably, those who get trapped in the hypocrisy syndrome find ways to mask their hollow core. The easiest approach is to add more activity, run faster, emphasize an intense, ever-enlarging agenda. The Pharisees were past masters at such things! Not content with the Mosaic Law that included the Ten Commandments, they tacked on 365 prohibitions, as well as 250 additional commandments. But did that make them righteous? Hardly.

> For I say to you, that unless your righteousness surpasses that of the scribes and Pharisees, you shall not enter the kingdom of heaven. (Matthew 5:20 NASB)

No, you didn't misread it; He said surpasses. You see, a busier schedule mixed with a longer to-do list does not equal greater righteousness any more than driving faster leads to a calmer spirit. On the contrary, when we attempt to become more spiritual by doing more things, we do nothing but complicate the Christian life. Can you imagine the shock on the faces of the Pharisees when they heard that Jesus was telling His followers that their righteousness must exceed that of the Pharisees?

In fact, if we do a quick overview of Jesus' magnificent message, we find Him simplifying the walk of faith with four basic teachings, all of which were diametrically opposed to the pharisaic lifestyle. First of all, He says:

Out with Hypocrisy! Even a casual reading through the forty-eight verses in the fifth chapter of Matthew leads me to believe Jesus is answering three questions:

1. What does it mean to have character? (verses 3–12)
2. What does it mean to make a difference? (verses 13–16)
3. What does it mean to be godly? (verses 17–48)

Interestingly, in that third section, verses 17–48, He repeats the same statement no fewer than six times:

> "You have heard . . . but I say to you. . . ." (verses 21–22)
> "You have heard . . . but I say to you. . . ." (verses 27–28)

"It was said . . . but I say to you. . . ." (verses 31–32 NASB)
"You have heard . . . but I say to you. . . ." (verses 33–34)
"You have heard . . . but I say to you. . . ." (verses 38–39 NASB)
"You have heard . . . but I say to you. . . ." (verses 43–44 NASB)

Why? What is Jesus getting at?

He is reminding the people of what they have heard for years, taught (and certainly embellished!) by their religious leaders; then He readdresses those same matters with an authentic life in view. And what kind of life is that? A life free of hypocrisy. Jesus' desire is that His followers be people of simple faith, modeled in grace, based on truth. Nothing more. Nothing less. Nothing else.

How easy it is to fake Christianity . . . to polish a superpious image that looks godly but is phony. Through the years I have come across Christians who are breaking their necks to be Mother Teresa Number Two or, if you please, Brother Teresa! Or Saint Francis of Houston or Minneapolis or Seattle . . . or wherever. Far too many Christians are simply trying too hard. They are busy, to be sure. But righteous? I mean, genuinely Christlike?

Sincere? Many of them. Intense? Most. Busy? Yes . . . but far from spiritual. . . .

Down with Performance! If the early part of Jesus' teaching is saying, "Out with hypocrisy," this next section, recorded in Matthew 6, is saying, "Down with performance!" Quit placing so much attention on looking good. Quit trying to make others think you are pious, especially if beneath the veneer there are hidden wickedness, impure motives, and shameful deeds. In other words, don't wear a smiling mask to disguise sadness and depravity, heartache and brokenness. In the area where I live, we would say, "Leave Showtime to the Los Angeles Lakers."

Jesus puts it straight: "Beware of practicing your righteousness before men to be noticed by them" (Matthew 6:1 NASB). In other words, "Stop acting one way before others, knowing you are really not that way at all." Then He offers three practical examples:

1. GIVING

When therefore you give alms [when you are in church and you give your money], do not sound a trumpet before you, as the hypocrites do in the synagogues and in the streets. (Matthew 6:2 NASB)

Today, we don't blow trumpets—not literally. But many who give sizable contributions like to see their names cast in bronze. They like it to be known by the public and remembered forever that they were the ones who built the gym. They are the ones who paid for the new organ. They are the heavy givers . . . the high donors: "A little extra fanfare, please." In contrast, when it came to giving, Jesus emphasized anonymity. No more hype, He said. When we live by simple faith, big-time performances that bring us the glory are out of place.

What a wonderful and welcome reminder—unless, of course, you are a religious glory hog. When we choose a life of simple faith, we keep our giving habits quiet.

2. PRAYING

And when you pray, you are not to be as the hypocrites; for they love to stand and pray in the synagogues and on the street corners, in order to be seen by men. Truly I say to you, they have their reward in full. But you, when you pray, go into your inner room, and when you have shut your door, pray to your Father who is in secret, and your Father who sees in secret will repay you. And when you are praying, do

not use meaningless repetition, as the Gentiles do, for they
suppose that they will be heard for their many words.
(Matthew 6:5–7 NASB)

Many words, even eloquent words, never caused anyone to be heard in prayer. . . .

Whatever happened to simplicity in prayer? And uncluttered honesty? Like the prayer of a child. Or the prayer of a humble farmer needing rain. Or of a homeless mother with two hungry kids. Down with performance-oriented praying! God honors simple-hearted petitions and humble-minded confession.

3. FASTING

And whenever you fast, do not put on a gloomy face as the
hypocrites do, for they neglect their appearance in order to
be seen fasting by men. Truly I say to you, they have their
reward in full. But you, when you fast, anoint your head,
and wash your face so that you may not be seen fasting by
men, but by your Father who is in secret; and your Father
who sees in secret will repay you. (Matthew 6:16–18 NASB)

This is a great place to stop and say a further word to fellow preachers. When it comes to piety performance, we can be the worst offenders! All preachers know there's a way to look and sound like The Reverend Supersanctified Saint of Ultrapious Cathedral or Dr. Dull Dryasdust with stooped shoulders, long face, and dark suit (an out-of-date tie also helps) . . . struggling to keep the tonnage of his world in orbit and its inhabitants in line. There's a great Greek word for that kind of nonsense: *Hogwash!* Jesus shot holes in that look-at-me-because-I'm-so-spiritual show-manship. If we choose to fast, fine. In fact, it's commendable. But if we fast (or counsel or study or pray) to be seen, forget it! These disciplines were never meant to be displays of the flesh. We are not in them for the grade others give us or the superficial impression we can make. Leave the acting to those who compete for the Emmys and the Oscars. . . . Let's keep it simple. Out with hypocrisy! Down with performance! And:

Up with Tolerance! I believe that is what Jesus is saying in the first five verses of Matthew 7 (NASB). What searching, convicting words these are!

> *Do not judge lest you be judged. For in the way you judge, you will be judged; and by your standard of measure, it will be measured to you. And why do you look at the speck that is in your brother's eye, but do not notice the log that is in your own eye? Or how can you say to your brother, "Let me take the speck out of your eye," and behold, the log is in your own eye? You hypocrite, first take the log out of your own eye, and then you will see clearly to take the speck out of your brother's eye.*

He is continuing His passionate, howling reproach against hypocrisy, isn't He? But have we taken Him seriously? Not nearly enough.

Christians are fast becoming "speck specialists." We look for specks and detect specks and criticize specks, all the while deliberately ignoring the much larger and uglier and more offensive logs in our own lives that need immediate attention and major surgery—in some cases, radical surgery.

May I get specific? Be tolerant of those who live different lifestyles. Be tolerant of those who don't look like you, who don't dress like you, who don't care about the things you care about, who don't relax like you, who don't vote like you. As my teenage kids used to ask each other, "Who died and put you in charge?" You're not their judge.

Let me go even further. Be tolerant of those whose fine points of theology differ from yours. Be tolerant of those whose worship style is different. Be tolerant even of those who have been turned off by Bible-thumping evangelicals—folks who are up to here with the pettiness and small-mindedness in many churches. Be tolerant of the young if you are older . . . and be tolerant of the aging if you are young. For those who are theologically astute (especially you who are gifted and trained linguistically), be tolerant of those who don't know Hebrew or Greek. There is certainly nothing wrong with knowing those languages, you understand. They can be extremely helpful. But they can also be misused and abused. People who don't know the original languages of Scripture can be taken advantage of by those who do. . . .

On with Commitment! Jesus' words penetrate, don't they? When our faith is a genuine faith—a simple expression of our walk with God—tolerance comes more easily. But does this negate commitment? Does everything about faith become passive and mildly indifferent? Not at all. Take a look at the rest of Jesus' talk recorded in Matthew 7. Pay close attention to the commands. Here are a few of them:

> *Do not give what is holy to dogs, and do not throw your pearls before swine, lest they trample them under their feet, and turn and tear you to pieces.*
>
> *Ask, and it shall be given to you; seek, and you shall find; knock, and it shall be opened to you. . . .*
>
> *Enter by the narrow gate; for the gate is wide, and the way is broad that leads to destruction, and many are those who enter by it. . . .*

Beware of the false prophets, who come to you in sheep's clothing, but inwardly are ravenous wolves. (Matthew 7:6–7, 13, 15 NASB)

Now that's commitment! . . .

As our Lord brings His teaching to a close, He tells the story of two houses, one built on rock and another built on sand. And with this He wraps up His words with one major statement: People of simple faith mean what they say and do what they hear. That, in essence, is the practical outworking of Christianity. That is simple faith in a nutshell.[1]

JESUS, YOUR TEACHER

Jesus was indeed a Master Communicator, a Master Teacher. He taught profound truths in a simple way. Everything he said was filtered through his winsome personality. No wonder the disciples gave up their careers to enroll in his course in practical theology! No wonder the crowds he taught constantly came back to hear more. He taught like no one they had ever heard. Unlike the rabbinical teachers of their day, Jesus did not cite famous Hebrew theologians in his lectures. He had no footnotes to divert his students' attention as they talked and listened. Jesus had no need to quote anyone other than himself.

Think about it: Jesus had three years to teach his followers what they would need to begin a movement that would change the world. (That's less time than most of us spent in high school!) Moreover, Jesus' students didn't come from the elite, knowledgeable, doctoral level folks who had plenty of background to build on. Instead, they came from the common people—fishermen, a tax collector, a zealot, and assorted other Jewish men. They knew the basics, for they had been through the synagogue training as all young Jewish boys had. They had a hunger; they were searching; their hearts were open.

For three years they followed Jesus, watching their Teacher interact with the crowds, observing miracles, listening to his words. They asked questions; Jesus asked them questions. They wondered. They surely talked much among themselves about who this man was and what the future held for them in their association with him. Often they misunderstood. In the end, when everything appeared to fall apart, they ran away.

But then, eleven of them "got it." Somewhere they remembered a glimmer of what Jesus had told them three separate times: "The Son of Man must be delivered into the hands of sinful men, and be crucified, and the third day rise again" (Luke 24:7). And when Jesus showed himself to them, their lives were forever changed. These men would go on to turn the world "upside down" (Acts 17:6).

What would it have been like to be with Jesus? Imagine sitting at the feet of the One who needed no notes to talk to you about the meaning of life. Don't you wish you could have been with the crowd that received the miraculous picnic from five loaves of bread and two fish? Wouldn't you have loved to have been in his small band of disciples, listening intently as he explained the meaning of a parable, receiving the power to preach and to heal, or simply being smiled at when he saw that you understood something he had said?

Have you ever wished you had been there? Wished that you could ask him about his will for your life—and have him *tell* you? Wished that your nagging question could be answered? Wished you could just lean on his chest, pouring out your tears, knowing that he understands your hurt, your pain, your fears, knowing that he can tell you what to do next?

Don't you wish that you, too, could learn from the Master Teacher?

Well, you can! God has made certain that you have the opportunity to learn from his Son. Jesus is indeed Teacher of the Ages, and he wants to be your Teacher today and every day. He has lessons for you to learn, questions to answer (and to ask!), and guidance to give. You will find Jesus the Teacher in his Word, in the wise words of other believers, and through the Holy Spirit.

READ GOD'S WORD

God has given his Word to give guidance and instructions to teach you how to live, how to think, how to trust, how to believe. You're never more than a page away from listening to Jesus. When you spend time in God's Word, you *are* in the presence of the Master Teacher. Even if you're not hearing his strong voice carry along a hillside in Galilee, you can still listen to Jesus. When you hold your Bible, you're holding the Savior's syllabus in your hands. Those who hung on his every word committed his life-changing words to paper.

The four Gospels tell us about Jesus' life, death, resurrection, and ascension. They record the words he taught. The rest of the New Testament tells the dramatic story of the first Christians as they absorbed the meaning of the events they had experienced with Jesus. Then, there are letters written by Peter, Paul, and other disciples, inspired by the Spirit of Christ, which encapsulate the bottom line of Jesus' message. But that's not all. The Old Testament provides the historical backdrop to explain the purpose for and meaning of Jesus' much-heralded entrance into history. In fact, "*All Scripture* is given by inspiration of God, and is profitable for doctrine, for reproof, for correction, for instruction in righteousness" (2 Timothy 3:16, italics added).

By daily reading of God's Word, you can sit at Jesus' feet and absorb the values of his Father's heart. You may not understand everything you read, but be patient and keep reading. The Holy Spirit will help you understand, for Scripture promises,

A person who does not have the Spirit does not accept the truths that come from the Spirit of God. That person thinks they are foolish and cannot understand them, because they can only be judged to be true by the Spirit. The spiritual person is able to judge all things, but no one can judge him. The Scripture says: "Who has known the mind of the Lord? Who has been able to teach him?" But we have the mind of Christ. (1 Corinthians 2:14–16 NCV)

ATTEND GOD'S CHURCH

When you sit in church and listen to a message based on God's Word, you are indirectly sitting at Jesus' feet being instructed by him. Those who open his book speak on his behalf. And just so we would be expectant when we gathered with other believers for the purpose of worship, Jesus reminded his followers that wherever two or more were gathered, he would be there too (Matthew 18:20). The reality of the first-century empty tomb guarantees that. When we quiet ourselves before the Word of God, the risen Christ monitors and coaches those "student teachers" who communicate for him.

Find a solid church with a pastor who preaches from God's Word. Take an example of the believers in Berea who, after listening to Paul and Silas preach, "searched the Scriptures daily to find out whether these things were so" (Acts 17:11).

You need the fellowship of other believers. Often Jesus' teachings will come to you through the words of a pastor, the conversation in a small group Bible study, or simply in a talk with a friend. The writer to the Hebrews said, "You should not stay away from the church meetings, as some are doing, but you should meet together and encourage each other. Do this even more as you see the day coming" (Hebrews 10:25 NCV).

OBEY THE SPIRIT'S PROMPTINGS

No matter how great a teacher is, he or she will not get through to a student who refuses to listen, who doesn't do the homework, who doesn't show up for class. The only way that favorite teacher you remember from school days made a difference in your life was because you listened carefully to his or her words and took the advice.

You want Jesus to truly be your Teacher? Then take very seriously what he teaches you. In short, we need to obey him.

Are you wondering what to do about a certain situation? When he shows you—through his Word or through the words of a pastor or Christian friend—then you would be wise to follow through. Are you worried about a concern in your life? Take that concern to him and then take seriously the words, "Be anxious for nothing, but in everything by prayer and supplication, with thanksgiving, let your requests be made known to God" (Philippians 4:6). Looking for guidance? Read, pray, watch. God is not out to deceive you; he's not trying to play games in order to keep you from knowing his will. He *wants* to show you, but he will do it *his* way in *his* time. He will begin to show you that passion in your heart; he will put you through his own training program; he will guide you a step at a time. Your job is to follow.

How will you hear that advice? That's the Holy Spirit's job. Jesus explained how his followers would be able to continue to hear from him by describing the One who would come: "The Spirit of truth, whom the world cannot receive, because it neither sees Him nor knows Him; but you know Him, for He dwells with you and will be in you" (John 14:17). Jesus went on, "But the Helper, the Holy Spirit, whom the Father will send in My name, He will teach you all things, and bring to your remembrance all things that I said to you" (John 14:26). The Holy Spirit will bring to mind the words you've read (provided you've been reading!).

He'll show you how those words apply to your current situation. He'll give you spiritual insight. He'll help you to hear and understand the Teacher's words.

Because Jesus was fully human, he knows what it's like to be tempted, to be hurt, to need guidance, to not know what the future holds. He wants to teach you how to live for him even as you face the difficulties of life on this earth. Sit at his feet and learn. Jesus, your Teacher, has a lesson for you—today and every day. "Jesus' desire is that His followers be people of simple faith, modeled in grace, based on truth. Nothing more. Nothing less. Nothing else."

Scripture Selections

ᘏ

Good and upright is the LORD;
Therefore He teaches sinners in the way.
The humble He guides in justice,
And the humble He teaches His way.
All the paths of the LORD are mercy and truth,
To such as keep His covenant and His testimonies.
For Your name's sake, O LORD,
Pardon my iniquity, for it is great.
Who is the man that fears the LORD?
Him shall He teach in the way He chooses.

PSALM 25:8–12

All your children shall be taught by the LORD,
And great shall be the peace of your children.

ISAIAH 54:13

Teach me Your way, O LORD,
And lead me in a smooth path, because of my enemies.

PSALM 27:11

I will instruct you and teach you in the way you should go;
I will guide you with My eye.

PSALM 32:8

O God, You have taught me from my youth;
And to this day I declare Your wondrous works.

PSALM 71:17

And so it was, when Jesus had ended these sayings, that the people were astonished at His teaching, for He taught them as one having authority, and not as the scribes.

MATTHEW 7:28–29

Many nations shall come and say,
"Come, and let us go up to the mountain of the LORD,
To the house of the God of Jacob;
He will teach us His ways,
And we shall walk in His paths."
For out of Zion the law shall go forth,
And the word of the LORD from Jerusalem.

MICAH 4:2

Then they went into Capernaum, and immediately on the Sabbath He entered the synagogue and taught. And they were astonished at His teaching, for He taught them as one having authority, and not as the scribes.

MARK 1:21–22

It is written in the prophets, "And they shall all be taught by God." Therefore everyone who has heard and learned from the Father comes to Me.

JOHN 6:45

You call me Teacher and Lord, and you say well, for so I am.

JOHN 13:13

Then He opens the ears of men, and seals their instruction.

JOB 33:16

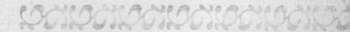

POEMS AND PRAYERS

ಞ

Gracious God, My Heart Renew

Gracious God, my heart renew,
Make my spirit right and true;
Cast me not away from Thee,
Let Thy Spirit dwell in me;
Thy salvation's joy impart,
Steadfast make my willing heart.

Sinners then shall learn from me
And return, O God, to Thee;
Savior, all my guilt remove,
And my tongue shall sing Thy love;
Touch my silent lips, O Lord,
And my mouth shall praise accord.
                        —*Author unknown*

Jesus, I've often wondered what it must have been like to have been a disciple. The Twelve must have reveled in their role as your pupils. I can almost smell the wildflowers on the grassy hillside on which they sat. Nonetheless, I'm grateful that you still delight in teaching people like me your ways. Open my heart and my mind to the things you have to teach me today. Amen.

FOR FURTHER THOUGHT

1. Describe a favorite teacher from your school or Sunday school days. What was it about this person's teaching that you liked?
2. How has Jesus given you guidance for decisions in your life?
3. In what ways have you seen Jesus teach you through your pastor and/or your friends?
4. In which area do you think you need the most improvement: spending time in God's Word, attending church, or obeying?
5. What do you need to do in order to be a better student of Jesus your Teacher?

For further reflection on Jesus as your Teacher, listen to "One Pure and Holy Passion" on the companion *Jesus* CD.

Jesus, the Healer

FEATURING THE WRITING OF SHEILA WALSH

Even a cursory look at the life of Jesus indicates that much of his three-year public ministry was spent dealing with individuals ravaged by sickness. Word spread throughout Israel that the woodworker from Nazareth could work miracles. Like a magnet, Jesus attracted those longing to see, hear, or walk. In almost every village he entered, those who were suffering sought him out. Children and adults. Men and women. People in pain longing for health reached out to be touched. And he touched even the untouchables—the lepers, the bleeding, those with diseases that made them outcasts.

Not one disease left Jesus intimidated or fearful. With uncanny accuracy he diagnosed every dilemma and confronted it. No untouchable sickness or vicious demon could cause the Son of God to shake in his sandals. And for good reason. He was aware that all power in heaven and on earth was at his fingertips. No matter the terror triggered by the mention of a horrible malady's name, he knew his name trumped all others. As the apostle Paul would later convey in his correspondence to the Philippians, Jesus' name is above every name, and at his name every knee must bow (Philippians 2:10). Diseases, too, bow before him.

People who were touched by Jesus went away healed, changed, and forgiven of their sins. The act of eliminating sickness was not an end in itself for Jesus. He knew that those who lived in an imperfect world would continue to contract any number of illnesses. The people he healed from blindness or deafness could still someday get a case of the flu. When he raised Lazarus from the dead, he knew it was only a temporary fix. His good friend from Bethany would eventually be buried again. Jesus made it clear that the reason he healed was to prove to those who witnessed his miracles that he was qualified to usher in the kingdom of God. It was Jesus' way of saying that he could heal *souls* as well as bodies. But lest we think that Jesus was only concerned with using his supernatural powers to validate his right to reign, we should take a look in his eyes. Those eyes that stared down the demon-possessed recluse in a graveyard also gave evidence of more than just messianic courage. They revealed love and compassion for those trapped by pain and humiliation. In each scene where Jesus healed the blind or allowed the lame to walk, there was tenderness and empathy. The Great Healer was genuinely moved with pity.

In other words, Jesus didn't just heal to make a point. He healed because his heart went out to those victimized by circumstances beyond their control. And you know what? He is still moved with compassion by those who long for wholeness and health. He still restores broken bodies, broken hearts, and wounded souls. Sheila Walsh knows that from experience. Listen as she tells her story.

READING FROM SHEILA WALSH

I have been in relationship with God since I was a young girl of eleven growing up in a small town on the west coast of Scotland.

My desire to please Him and respond to that love led me through Bible college to roles as a youth evangelist, contemporary Christian artist, and television host on the Christian Broadcasting Network.

But after working side by side with Dr. Pat Robertson and the staff of *The 700 Club* for five years, I was admitted as a patient in the psychiatric wing in a hospital in Washington, D.C., diagnosed with severe clinical depression. I felt as if I was drowning, dragged under the water by rocks of despair, sadness, and hopelessness. I had no issue with God. I believed then and believe now that God is good and loving and kind. The issue was with me. I was disenchanted with all the efforts of Sheila Walsh. I was dizzy from years of trying to keep all the plates spinning in the air in an attempt to show God how much I loved Him. Nothing I did felt as if it was enough.

Have you been there? Are you there right now?

For years I had taken comfort in the omission of the "big sins" in my life. I thought that if I were a "good girl," then God would love me more. I was sexually pure and abstained from anything that was on my long list of things to avoid if I wanted God to be happy with me. As I moved into my thirties, that comfort blanket had worn thin. I saw in myself the potential for disaster of every kind. I saw hypocrisy and fear; I felt anger and resentment. I had worked so hard to be approved by God and by others. I was finally tired of it all.

The plates began to smash around me. Depression seemed to invade my body like the beginning of a long, dark winter. By that fall of 1992, I felt as if I was getting colder and colder inside every day. My decision to check into a psych ward was based on the simple fact that I had tried everything else that was familiar to me, everything I knew to do, but nothing made a difference.

I had tried to eat better and exercise more. I had fasted and prayed for twenty-one days. I had worked harder and longer than ever. Yet this invasion of frosty hopelessness gained ground. The hospital was a last resort and a dreaded one. When he was in his midthirties, my father died in a psychiatric hospital, and I wondered if I had inherited his fate just as surely as I had been gifted with his brown eyes.

Some of my friends were horrified that as a Christian, I would consider reaching out for this kind of help. They offered the more traditional remedies. Perhaps you have received a similar prescription.

People told me to pray more, confess any unconfessed sin, listen to more praise music, get involved in helping someone who was in a worse state than I was, paste verses of Scripture to the dashboard in my car—the list went on and on. What some of my advisors didn't know was that I had tried all of those things many, many times. I found the list heartbreaking. The implication was clear: the problem was with my spiritual life. That only added to the guilt that I already carried.

My family was very supportive. My mom urged me to have courage to walk through this dark night. She assured me that God was with me and would walk with me every step of the way. I heard her words but they slipped through the cracks of a broken heart.

Just before I was admitted to the hospital in Washington, I was driving home from work when a storm appeared out of nowhere. The sky turned black, and lightning slashed the sky in two. It was as if an aqueduct opened in the clouds and dumped plaguelike rain on the tarmac. I thought that it was my fault. I thought that God was angry with me. Even as I write that, I find it hard to imagine myself in such a place, but when I was overwhelmed with guilt and shame, it seemed as if everything that was wrong with the world was *my* fault.

Some of my friends told me that what I was doing was spiritual and professional suicide. They said that when people learned that I had been in a psychiatric institution, I would never be trusted again as a broadcaster or as a believer. I was sure that they were right, but I didn't need a public relations company at that moment. I needed a place to fall on my face before the throne of God and hear what He had to say.

I don't know what I expected from this temporary prison, but I could never have imagined what God would do in me in this place of my undoing. Even as I ran out of mercy for myself, His mercy overwhelmed me, and His compassion began to change my life moment by moment, cell by cell. I discovered that the faint hope I had in the solutions my friends offered me was nothing compared to the absolute hope offered by Christ. I want you to know that Christ has changed my life. It didn't happen overnight. I am not a fan of quick fixes or imagined healing. What Jesus has done for me has totally changed everything in my life. He taught me how to live. . . .

It was the beginning of my healing. I began to read God's Word and hear Him talk to *me,* not just find a verse that might encourage someone else. As I read verses that talked about God as Father, I took comfort in that name. It was such a relief. For years I had worked harder and harder to make God like me. Finally I began to understand not only does He like me but how passionately He loves me. As my life moved on, I began to see how others struggle with the very same issues. . . .

LONGING TO BE HEALED

We are wounded by life, by each other, by our poor choices or the poor choices of others.

We long to be healed from those wounds, to be free, to be whole.

At moments we experience a glimpse of healing from God, and yet we seem to be able to lose it in a moment—another careless word, a disappointment with ourselves or with others. So what are we to do? . . .

Is there lasting healing on this earth, or are we doomed to simply patch ourselves up as best we can until we finally limp home to the arms of our Father in heaven?

I am learning that God's overwhelming love gives us the courage and grace to look at our wounds, no matter how deep or painful they are, and to bring them out of the dark into His light. Perhaps as you think of your wounds, God's love seems absent. You might ask,

"Where were You, God, when these things were happening to me?"

"Where were You, God, when some of life's deepest wounds were being inflicted?"

"Do You see?"

"Do You care?"

These are valid questions and ones we will think about together, but let me say at this point, the same God who holds the universe in place loves you. Perhaps that is where you struggle, not wondering where God was, but questioning that God could love you in spite of where you have been. I believe that God loves you right now with all that is true about your life—externally and internally. That's my life message. It's a message that we can never hear too many times, for it contradicts the thunderous voices of dissent in our heads. Those voices tell us that it can't possibly be true, not with all we know about ourselves and all that has been done to us. We know that we have failed to reach God's standards. We know that we have failed in our relationships with each other, so how can a holy and pure God possibly love us with no reserve?

It took me a long time to be able to receive God's love, to believe that His love is as constant on my bad days as on my ducks-in-a-row days. I believe it now with all my heart and soul.

That may be hard for you to accept for yourself right now.

I began to ask God to help me understand how we are to live in this world with all the potential for hurt, pain, and fear and yet experience a deep healing that we are able to hold onto, no matter what life throws at us. . . .

The Lamb of God gave everything He could give to restore our battered souls and place joy and light back into the darkened rooms of our hearts. It's time to come out of the shadows, remove the masks, and stop hiding. He invites us now to walk with Him, fight side by side with Him, and love with Him. . . .

GOD SENT A HEALER

I want you to know that you are not alone, that hope and healing are to be found in Christ. There *is* a way out of your pit. It's not an immediate thing; it is a process, but it is available to you.

You begin by simply being open to healing. I believe that because of God's grace and mercy, you can bring each one of the painful snapshots of your past into Christ's light. You can put them on the table and look at them with Jesus right by your side. That's where you begin. I don't believe that the Holy Spirit simply takes an eraser and removes all the marks of pain from your heart but rather He gives you the grace to face each moment in the company of your Savior.

Christ carried the scars of the Crucifixion with Him as He rose from the dead but the wounds were healed. They were not festering in the darkness. Wounds that are left untreated or covered over don't heal as they should.

I have had the thumb on my right hand broken three times. The first time it happened I was working on a summer youth mission in England and didn't bother having it looked at. The bone healed but it healed crookedly and has remained vulnerable to further damage and pain if someone accidentally twists it.

The wounds on Christ's hands and side healed in such a way that He could offer them to Thomas, the one who doubted, as proof that He was indeed Jesus, the risen Christ. He didn't hide His wounds or have them erased. They are part of His identity.

I will always carry the scar of the loss of my father, but it is no longer a weeping wound. Christ has removed the poison and all that is left is the mark. Jesus wants you to bring your festering wounds into His light so that He can heal them to be touched by others.

There are many negative images to erase along the way, but you can start. You can take just one step and ask God to help you to be willing to have your wounds brought into His healing light.

When I am afraid or uncertain I turn to God's Word.

You, O God the Lord,
Deal with me for Your name's sake;
Because Your mercy is good, deliver me.
For I am poor and needy,
And my heart is wounded within me. (Psalm 109:21–22)

Restore to me the joy of Your salvation,
And uphold me by Your generous Spirit. (Psalm 51:12)

. . . Into our weary world, our shattered dreams, and broken hearts God sent a healer. He was a healer in disguise. You would need to be desperate to find Him, but to those who are desperate, He is here!

God saw that we were stuck and gave birth to the answer: "For God so loved the world that He gave His only begotten Son, that whoever believes in Him should not perish but have everlasting life" (John 3:16).

I have known this verse since I was a child in Sunday school. It is probably the first verse I ever memorized. It's a verse full of life and meaning.

The Greek word used here for "everlasting" refers not only to how long we will live but also to the quality of life we live right now, as contrasted with a sense of hopelessness. Everlasting, or eternal, life is a deepening and growing experience every day. It can never be exhausted. It speaks of a new quality of life. *We are not saved to simply make it through this world until we are finally home free. Christ died to give us life, life right now.* Are you experiencing that? If, like me, you are longing to be in relationship with the only One who sees all our brokenness and longs to bring healing and hope, may I remind you that there is such a One? His name is Jesus. . . .

LONGING FOR GOD

Whether we are looking for signs and wonders, physical healing, or a balm for our wounded souls, underneath it all we are longing for God. We might not recognize that, but we are made to be in intimate relationship with Him. When we are not, we try to fill that void with whatever we perceive to be our greatest felt need. Underneath it all we want God to be real to us, to touch us.

God moves in many different ways, and who am I to say what God will do for anyone or how He might choose to manifest His presence? I have learned enough to know that God's ways and thoughts are outside my human capacity for reason. What troubles me, though, is that we seek what God might *do* instead of seeking God Himself. What troubles me is that we are more after God's hand than God's face.

You could have every tooth in your head turn to gold, but what would it profit you in the long run? What we need is heart surgery.

We need God to heal our broken hearts. God could heal your body, but if your heart is still full of pain, bitterness, and disappointment, the healing is limited to what would show up in an X-ray.

God asks that we be hungry for Him, seek Him, kneel down and roll our burdens onto Him. The greatest gift that you and I can give ourselves is to fall in love with Jesus. Everything else in this life is temporary; only life with Him has any lasting meaning. *Let's not occupy our lives chasing after the latest craze; let's chase after God who is crazy about us. . . .*

A TIME FOR HEALING

It's time to invite Christ into these broken places and let Him make us whole. Let's consider what the psalmist David said as he cried out to God:

> *Have mercy on me, O LORD, for I am weak;*
> *O LORD, heal me, for my bones are troubled.*
> *My soul also is greatly troubled;*
> *But You, O LORD—how long?*
> *Return, O LORD, deliver me!*
> *Oh, save me for Your mercies' sake! (Psalm 6:2–4)*

> *The sacrifices of God are a broken spirit,*
> *A broken and a contrite heart—*
> *These, O God, You will not despise. (Psalm 51:17)*

You might find it helpful to get a journal or a notebook and write down what the Spirit of God brings to mind. Beside each entry of pain or sadness, covering each wound, you can write:

> *He was wounded for our transgressions,*
> *He was bruised for our iniquities;*

The chastisement for our peace was upon Him,
And by His stripes we are healed. (Isaiah 53:5)

His punishment is meant to bring us peace; His wounds bring us healing.

Some of your wounds may be so great and so painful that it would be wise to find a godly counselor to help you deal with them. Your pastor may be available to help or refer you to someone who can walk with you. There are counselors who deal specifically with sexual abuse, with eating disorders, with rape trauma. Don't be ashamed to ask for help, and don't be put off until you find the right person to help you. Jesus gave His life for you. You are worth saving!

If you struggle with depression, situational or genetic, there is great help available. I have been on the drug Zoloft for more than ten years and have found it to be a gift from God. The church is divided on the use of psychiatric medicine and even psychiatric counseling. . . . Let me just say here, though, *if you need help, get help.* Don't be ashamed to reach out and take the help that is available. *God wants you restored, strong, and full of His life and love.*

That might be a little scary at first. We can become used to having a broken heart. Whether our broken hearts are a result of things that have been done to us, such as abuse or tragic loss, or whether we struggle with depression and anxiety that can be genetically inherited, the effect on the heart is the same. Only Christ can heal us.

Jesus once asked a man, "Do you want to get well?" The man in question had been sick for a long time. He was identified by it; people recognized him as the one who could do nothing to help himself. Jesus' question required a lot of him. Healing in this case happened in a moment, but he would have to live out the rest of his life making different choices. When he lay by the pool, those who passed him might have thrown some coins toward his plight or a kind word, a moment of sympathy and human connection. If he was healed, he must become part of the healing of others.

Being healed by Christ teaches you one thing for sure: we are healed to come to others in Jesus' name, offering the same healing. We are no longer at liberty to be part of the problem; we are given the joy of being part of the solution. Do you want to get well? Those who have been broken and restored by Christ have a God-given ability to connect with others in pain and offer hope and healing. It is one of the greatest privileges of my life to watch the way God uses what was a nightmare to me at the time as a candle in the darkness to others.

When Christ heals us, when we get up and walk again, we discover there is work to be done. We have begun to live again! . . .

FIND REAL HEALING IN JESUS

Real healing is offered to you if you will come to Jesus, just as you are right now. It's easy to believe that God is love, so therefore God must love me. But I like Brennan Manning's question in *The Wisdom of Tenderness:* "Do I wholeheartedly trust that God likes me? And do I trust that God likes me, not after I clean up my act and eliminate every trace of sin, . . . but in this moment, right now, right here, with all my faults and weaknesses?"

If you answer yes, then you are living in the grace of those whose hearts have been broken, crucified, and resurrected by a living Lord Jesus.

I plead with you in the name of the Wounded Healer who gave everything so that we could live, come to Jesus, and live a life worth living.

In Jesus alone, there is real healing.[1]

JESUS, YOUR HEALER

Real healing is found in Jesus alone. The same eyes of compassion that looked into the eyes of first-century victims of disease and abuse are focused in your direction as well. He knows the fear you wrestle with, prompted by a doctor's diagnosis. He sees the relational bruises you admit to only in private. He feels the emotional pain you endure in silence. He knows the addictions that suffocate you. He wants to heal you.

The writer to the Hebrews celebrates the fact that "our high priest is able to understand our weaknesses. When he lived on earth, he was tempted in every way that we are, but he did not sin" (Hebrews 4:15 NCV). The author goes on to say that Jesus (as our high priest in heaven) continually intercedes for us by asking God to help us (Hebrews 7:25).

Visualize Jesus, your high priest, seated in heaven. But don't stop there. Knowing his caring concern as well as his life-changing power, imagine yourself seated in his presence. Mindful of his healing touch when he was on earth and his intercession on your behalf now, you can begin to benefit from the ministry of healing he continues to offer. That healing comes as you participate in his "treatment plan."

ACKNOWLEDGE YOUR NEED

When you're sick, it's dangerous to pretend that you are healthier than you really are. You need to acknowledge your need, admit the truth, and resist the tendency to cover up.

The same is true with the illnesses—physical or emotional— you may bring to Jesus. You must verbalize your plight in prayer. Don't pretend to be well; don't think you can hide the truth from him. He already knows your situation, and he wants you to express it yourself. Full disclosure is the first step to reaching the destination of wholeness.

When Jesus passed through the ancient town of Jericho en route to Jerusalem, a blind beggar named Bartimaeus heard that Jesus was approaching. At that moment, his begging took on a different form. Instead of crying out for money, he cried out for the Master's touch. "Jesus, son of David, have mercy on me!" Bartimaeus blurted out (see Mark 10:48). Jesus could tell the man wanted his sight, but in order for the man to cooperate in his healing, Jesus asked him, "What do you want me to do for you?" Wasting no time, Bartimaeus responded, "Teacher, I want to see" (Mark 10:51 NCV).

Do you need physical healing? Perhaps a doctor has given you a limited time to live. Maybe you've just been diagnosed with a painful, debilitating, or terminal disease. Tell the Lord that you're scared. Ask for his guidance in seeking treatment.

Do you need mental healing? Perhaps you need some kind of medication to alleviate your depression. Or perhaps you've been diagnosed with a bipolar condition or other form of illness that, while not terminal, is just as frightening. Ask the One who created you what he would have you do in order to live in wholeness.

Do you struggle with addictions to alcohol or painkillers or anything else? You need to admit that you have a problem. You need to ask the Lord what you can do to come clean before him.

Is your pain rooted in relational conflict? Though not based in anything physical, a bruised relationship can often manifest itself in physical symptoms like stress, headaches, or sleeplessness. Admit to the Lord that you need his help to seek reconciliation.

Whatever you're facing today, acknowledge that you need the Healer to walk with you through the dark days ahead.

TAKE YOUR MEDICINE

When you've described your symptoms to your doctor, he pulls out a tablet and writes a prescription. Once he's heard you say you're not well, he seeks to relieve your discomfort and facilitate healing. By admitting your need to the Lord, you are in a position to listen to his advice and take the medicine he gives you.

When Jesus encountered ten lepers on a rural road, he pronounced them cured but then told them to go show themselves to the local priest (Luke 17:12–14). When he revived a twelve-year-old girl from death, he instructed her parents to give her something to eat (Mark 5:41–43). In each case Jesus had a reason for his request: compliance with his instructions was a tangible way of acknowledging dependence on God.

What is the Healer asking you to do? If he knows that your ultimate physical healing will not be realized this side of heaven, he may be asking you to make sure your will is up to date and in order. He may be prompting you to make peace with that person who has done you wrong (or whom you offended). If you're struggling with stress, he may desire you to follow your doctor's orders for increased rest, a healthier diet, and regular exercise.

But Jesus also calls you to spend time in his presence. He invited all who labor and are heavy laden to come to him and rest (Matthew 11:28–30). Sometimes holding on to the truth that the Lord delights in being with you is the very best medicine you can swallow. Ask him what he wants you to do in the situation you're facing. What prescription is the Healer writing for you today?

FOLLOW THE PRESCRIBED REGIMEN

Often your doctor will prescribe a treatment program that includes more than medication; he may require some kind of regimen on your part involving diet or exercise. If you have a back problem, your therapy will include stretching and bending. If your muscles have grown weak through atrophy, the doctor may ask you to lift weights. If you need to take off some excess weight in order to help your heart, he will prescribe a healthy diet.

To experience Jesus' healing touch, you would do well to consider certain exercises as well. Three important exercises to follow to stay close to God are Bible reading, prayer, and involvement in an accountability group.

For example, as you search for healing, read the accounts in the Gospels where Jesus touched the afflicted and responded to their cries for help. Picture yourself in the story. Hear the voices of the crowds. Taste the dust in the air from the foot traffic on the hot unpaved paths. Feel the touch of the Savior's hand. Allow the recounting of this true event to fuel your faith.

Then pray the Scriptures. In your reading, when you come to a truth that speaks of Jesus' power or the comfort he promises to give, verbalize that truth to the Lord in the form of a prayer. For example, when the apostle Paul was struggling with personal difficulties, he explained his faith to the Philippian Christians, "I can do all things through Christ who strengthens me" (Philippians 4:13). What was true for him can be true for you. Pray that Scripture by saying something like, "Jesus, I want to thank you that in spite of the problems that plague my life, you are willing to give me strength that I can cope today."

Another exercise would be to meet regularly with a small group of believers. The purpose of this exercise is to know the loving support of other people who can hold you accountable, pray for you, and encourage you. Their ability to help out tangibly will help to lighten your load.

REMEMBER THAT HIS GRACE IS ENOUGH

Jesus' goal is always to bring people to salvation and to bring glory to the Father. He does indeed still provide complete physical and emotional healing to people at times. He will work through doctors and medicines and prescribed regimens in order to bring sick people back to health—and we should always avail ourselves of those options. (When King Hezekiah was sick and asked for healing from the prophet Isaiah, God sent Isaiah back with some medicine! Read the story in 2 Kings 20:1–7.) Clearly, God works through those kinds of helps to bring people back to strength and wholeness.

At times, however, a plea for healing will be answered negatively. The apostle Paul experienced this. Listen as he explains:

A painful physical problem was given to me. . . . I begged the Lord three times to take this problem away from me. But he said to me, "My grace is enough for you. When you are weak, my power is made perfect in you." So I am very happy to brag about my weaknesses. Then Christ's power can live in me. For this reason I am happy when I have weaknesses, insults, hard times, sufferings, and all kinds of troubles for Christ. Because when I am weak, then I am truly strong. (2 Corinthians 12:7–10 NCV)

It didn't make sense to Paul, so he pled with God to take away the physical problem. After all, it was apparently debilitating. Couldn't Paul have been more effective in sharing the gospel without that illness plaguing him at times? What makes sense to us may not be in God's plan at all. God said no to Paul, and Paul was willing to accept that answer because he knew God's grace would be enough.

Whatever type of illness or pain you may be facing today, Jesus the Healer is right there with you. His grace is enough for you. Ask God to glorify himself through you. And remember the promise of the future that, one day, we will all be healed completely. Jesus the Healer will make all things new. In his future kingdom, "He will wipe away every tear . . . and there will be no more death, sadness, crying, or pain, because all the old ways are gone" (Revelation 21:4 NCV).

Scripture Selections

ಞಞ

*"But that you may know that the Son of Man has power on earth
to forgive sins"—He said to the paralytic, "I say to you, arise,
take up your bed, and go to your house."*

MARK 2:10–11

*The Spirit of the LORD is upon Me,
Because He has anointed Me
To preach the gospel to the poor;
He has sent Me to heal the brokenhearted,
To proclaim liberty to the captives
And recovery of sight to the blind,
To set at liberty those who are oppressed.*

LUKE 4:18

*He heals the brokenhearted
And binds up their wounds.*

PSALM 147:3

*Heal me, O LORD, and I shall be healed;
Save me, and I shall be saved,
For You are my praise.*

JEREMIAH 17:14

*Bless the LORD, O my soul,
And forget not all His benefits:
Who forgives all your iniquities,
Who heals all your diseases.*

PSALM 103:2–3

Now a woman, having a flow of blood for twelve years, who had spent all her livelihood on physicians and could not be healed by any, came from behind and touched the border of His garment. And immediately her flow of blood stopped.

LUKE 8:43–44

When He was reviled, did not revile in return; when He suffered, He did not threaten, but committed Himself to Him who judges righteously; who Himself bore our sins in His own body on the tree, that we, having died to sins, might live for righteousness—by whose stripes you were healed.

1 PETER 2:23–24

But He was wounded for our transgressions,
He was bruised for our iniquities;
The chastisement for our peace was upon Him,
And by His stripes we are healed.

ISAIAH 53:5

My people who are called by My name will humble themselves, and pray and seek My face, and turn from their wicked ways, then I will hear from heaven, and will forgive their sin and heal their land.

2 CHRONICLES 7:14

In the middle of its street, and on either side of the river, was the tree of life, which bore twelve fruits, each tree yielding its fruit every month. The leaves of the tree were for the healing of the nations.

REVELATION 22:2

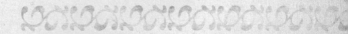

POEMS AND PRAYERS

ɞɔɕ

My Faith Has Found a Resting Place

My faith has found a resting place,
Not in device or creed;
I trust the ever living One,
His wounds for me shall plead.

Enough for me that Jesus saves,
This ends my fear and doubt;
A sinful soul I come to Him,
He'll never cast me out.

My heart is leaning on the Word,
The living Word of God,
Salvation by my Savior's Name,
Salvation through His blood.

My great Physician heals the sick,
The lost He came to save;
For me His precious blood He shed,
For me His life He gave.

I need no other argument,
I need no other plea,
It is enough that Jesus died,
And that He died for me.

—Eliza E. Hewitt

Jesus, I need your healing today. The sickness I face needs your intervention. Show me what I should do. You created me; you know that this is in my life. Show me now what course I need to take to be brought back to wholeness. And if this sickness is going to end in my death, show me what I need to do to prepare those I love. You promise that your grace is enough, Jesus. I need that grace today. Glorify yourself through my life. Amen.

FOR FURTHER THOUGHT

1. In what area(s) of your life do you need Jesus' healing touch today?
2. In what ways have you sought his guidance and presence?
3. What "prescription" has Jesus written for you to begin your healing process? Have you been taking his advice?
4. How would you advise or encourage someone who has received a "no" to his or her request for physical healing?
5. In what ways can you glorify Jesus, even through your illness?

For further reflection on Jesus as your Healer, listen to "All Who Are Thirsty" on the companion *Jesus* CD.

Jesus, the Prince of Peace

FEATURING THE WRITING OF BILLY GRAHAM

I n the first century the relatively peaceful security that blan-
keted the Roman Empire was called Pax Romana. That peace (*pax*
in Latin) was made possible by provincial leaders loyal to Rome, a
common language, passable roads, and a standing army ready to
deal quickly and decisively with any insurrection. In other words,
except in times of upheaval or war, an atmosphere of peace pre-
vailed throughout the empire of the Caesars. Like any worldly
peace, however, the Pax Romana was tenuous at best. While it
offered great prosperity to some, it brought misery to others. While
some enjoyed its benefits, others groaned under the weight of
oppression. Peace, maybe, but not perfect peace.

Jesus offers something very different, although the people of his
day didn't understand it. When Jesus entered Jerusalem on a donkey,
the people went wild. Here was their king who would usher in a new
golden age for Israel and bring them peace and freedom from the
oppression of Rome. Here was their king who would set them free.

They soon learned that they had it wrong—at least at that

moment. One day Jesus *will* return and bring peace to the world, but that wasn't what his first coming was all about. He came not in order to overthrow kingdoms, but to overthrow sin in people's hearts. He came to bring inner peace, a resource on which to draw no matter what our outside circumstances. It was not peace like Rome tried to provide. No—it was far better! "Peace I leave with you, My peace I give to you; not as the world gives do I give to you. Let not your heart be troubled, neither let it be afraid" (John 14:27).

An illustration of this kind of peace is recorded in the Gospels. Jesus and his disciples were sailing from one side of the Sea of Galilee to the other following a long day of ministry. Jesus, weary from the events of the day, was dead tired. Curling up in a corner of the small boat, he fell asleep. So deep was his sleep that he was oblivious to a raging storm that developed. The winds were blowing with gale-force strength; the waves were crashing over the sides. Understandably, the disciples began to panic and fear for their lives.

Jesus continued to sleep peacefully—at least until they woke him up and demanded that he do something! So he did. "He arose and rebuked the wind, and said to the sea, 'Peace, be still!' And the wind ceased and there was a great calm." (Read the story in Mark 4:35–41.)

Are you struck by the irony of this scenario? Although unsettling circumstances were rocking his world, Jesus was at peace. Take it to the next level. Not only was Jesus unconcerned with the life-threatening crisis, his presence in the storm-rocked vessel guaranteed that the boat would not go down. As long as Jesus was on board, the disciples were safe. His presence brought peace.

Jesus certainly never promised a storm-free existence. In fact, his invitation to the abundant life assumes there will be combat, risk, and adventure (see the chapter on Jesus, the Mighty Warrior). What he did promise was his presence. And with the promise of his companionship comes the ability to rest assured that he is in control. He told his followers, "These things I have spoken to you, that in Me you may have peace. In the world you will have tribulation; but be of good cheer, I have overcome the world" (John 16:33).

Billy Graham shows that only with Jesus in your life can you truly experience peace. Only then will you understand why he is called the Prince of Peace.

READING FROM BILLY GRAHAM

THE GREAT QUEST

You started on the Great Quest the moment you were born. It was many years perhaps before you realized it, before it became apparent that you were constantly searching—searching for something you'd never had, searching for something that was more important than anything else in life.

Sometimes you have tried to forget about the quest. Sometimes you have attempted to lose yourself in other things so there could be time and thought for nothing but the business at hand. Sometimes you may even have felt that you were freed from the need to go on searching for this nameless thing. But always you have been caught up in it again; always you have had to come back to your search.

You Are Not Alone. At the loneliest moments in your life you have looked at other men and women and wondered if they, too, were searching—searching for something they couldn't describe but knew they wanted and needed. Looking at them you may have thought, *These people are not on the Great Quest. These people have found their way.*

Not so! You are not alone. All people are traveling with you, for everyone is on this same quest. All people are seeking the answer to the confusion, the moral sickness, the spiritual emptiness that oppresses the world. We are all crying out for guidance, for comfort, for happiness, for peace.

We are told that we live in the "age of anxiety." Seldom in history have people faced so much fear and uncertainty. All the familiar props seem to have been knocked out from under us. We talk of peace but are confronted by war and terrorism at every turn. We devise elaborate schemes for security but have not found it. We grasp at every passing straw, and even as we clutch, it disappears.

For generations we have been running like frightened children, up first one blind alley and then another. Each time we have told ourselves, *This path is the right one; this one will take us where we want to go.* But each time we have been wrong.

The Happiness Illusion. We all recognize that the world has changed radically in the last one hundred years. We are aware of its increasing tempo, of the spirit of revolution that is sweeping away established landmarks and traditions, of the speed with which language, fashions, customs, housing, and our ways of living and thinking are being altered.

Our materialistic world rushes on with its eternal quest for happiness. Yet the more knowledge we acquire, the less wisdom we seem to have. The more economic security we gain, the more bored and insecure we become. The more everyday pleasure we enjoy, the less satisfied and contented we are with life. We are like a restless sea, rushing in waves toward a little peace here and a little pleasure there but finding nowhere to stay that's permanent and satisfying.

Yet inside us a little voice keeps saying, *We were not meant to be this way; we were meant for better things.* We have a feeling that there must be a fountain somewhere that contains the happiness that makes life worthwhile. Sometimes we feel we have obtained it—only to find it elusive, leaving us disillusioned, bewildered, unhappy, and still searching.

There are two kinds of happiness. One comes to us when our circumstances are pleasant and we are relatively free from troubles. The problem is that this kind of happiness is fleeting and superficial. When circumstances change—as they inevitably do—this kind of happiness evaporates like the early morning fog in the heat of the mid-day sun.

But there is another kind of happiness—the kind for which we all long and search. This second kind of happiness is a lasting inner joy and peace that survive any circumstance. It's a happiness that endures, no matter what comes our way. Oddly, it may even grow stronger in adversity.

The happiness for which our hearts ache is one undisturbed by success or failure, one which dwells deep within us and gives inward peace and contentment, no matter what the surface problems may be. It's the kind of happiness that stands in need of no outward stimulus.

This is the kind of happiness we need. This is the happiness for which our souls cry out and search relentlessly.

Is there any hope for this kind of happiness? Is there any way out of our dilemma? Can we really find personal peace?

Yes! But only if we look in the right place.

FINDING THE WAY BACK

If I could come and have a heart-to-heart chat with you in your living room, you might confess, "I am perplexed, confused, and mixed up. I have broken God's laws. I have lived contrary to His commandments. I thought I could get along without God's help. I've tried to make up my own rules, and I've failed. What I would give to be born again! What I would give to go back and start all over—what a different road I'd travel if I could!"

If those words strike a familiar chord in your heart, I want to tell you some glorious news. Jesus said you can be born again! You can have the fresh start for which you've longed. You can become a new person—a clean and peaceful person from whom sin has been washed away.

A Way Out. No matter how soiled your past or snarled your present, no matter how hopeless your future seems to be—there is a way out. There is a sure, safe, everlasting way out, but there is only one way! That way is Jesus Christ, who said, "I am the way, and the truth, and the life. The only way to the Father is through me" (John 14:6).

You can go on being miserable, discontented, frightened, unhappy, and disgusted with yourself, or you can decide right now that you want to be born again. You can have your sinful past wiped out and make a new start, a fresh start, a right start. You can decide now to become the person that Jesus promised you could be.

How Can I Be Born Again? The next question you may ask is, "How can I have this rebirth? How can I be born again? How can I start afresh?"

Here are some guidelines from the Bible that will help you be born again by accepting Christ as your Lord and Savior:

First, you must recognize what God did. He loved you so much He gave His Son to die on the cross for you. We discussed that in Chapter 6 of this book.

Second, you must repent of your sins. Jesus said that unless you repent, you will die (Luke 13:3). It's not enough just to be sorry. Repent means to turn away from sin—to change your heart and life.

Third, by faith you must receive Jesus Christ as Savior and commit yourself to Him as Lord. This means that you stop trying to save yourself and accept Christ as your only Lord and Savior.

John 1:12 says, "To all who did accept him and believe in him he gave the right to become children of God." Trust Him completely, without reservation. Do it now!

Get on Board! Let's say you decide to fly to Europe. You contact your travel agent, make reservations, and buy your ticket. You pack your bags and take a taxi to the airport. You even check your bags, get your boarding pass, and walk to the gate. But if you stop there, you'll never make it to Europe. Why? One thing is lacking: You need to get on board the plane!

To know *about* Christ is not enough. To be convinced that He is the Savior of the world is not enough. To affirm our belief in Him is not enough. To believe that He has saved others is not enough. We really don't believe in Christ until we make a *commitment* of our lives to Him and by faith receive Him as our Savior. We have to get on board with Jesus!

Why not get on board *today*? The Bible says, "The 'right time' is now, and the 'day of salvation' is now" (2 Corinthians 6:2). If you are willing to repent of your sins and to receive Jesus Christ as your Lord and Savior, you can do it right now.

How to Begin. You may say, "I really want to be born again, but how do I begin?" I would suggest that you make a list of all your sins. Then confess them to God one by one and check them off, remembering that Jesus Christ has promised to forgive. Hold nothing back! Give them all to Jesus. The Bible says, "If we confess our sins, he will forgive our sins. . . . He will cleanse us from all the wrongs we have done" (1 John 1:9).

Next, ask God to cleanse you from those sins you may not be aware of and to make you more sensitive to hidden sins in your life—wrong motives, wrong attitudes, wrong habits, wrong relationships, wrong priorities. You may even need to make restitution if you have stolen anything, or you may need to seek out someone and ask forgiveness for a wrong you have committed.

In this way you "die to your sins" and share in Christ's death on the cross for you. The apostle Paul said, "I was put to death on the cross with Christ, and I do not live anymore—it is Christ who lives in me" (Galatians 2:20).

Your Response. At this moment I invite you either to bow your head or get on your knees and say this prayer:

O God, I admit that I have sinned against You. I am sorry for my sins. I am willing to turn from my sins. I openly receive and trust Jesus Christ as my Savior. I confess Him as my Lord. From this moment on I want to live for Him and serve Him in the fellowship of His church. In Jesus' name. Amen.

I believe that Jesus Christ is the Son of the Living God. I commit myself to Him as the Lord and Savior of my life.

Signed —————————————————————

Date —————————————————————

If you sincerely prayed this prayer, my friend, then welcome home! Welcome into the love and fellowship of the family of God.

PEACE AT LAST

One of the powerful, enduring images that my wife, Ruth, and I have of our early years together is of the ticker-tape parades in New York City celebrating the end of World War II. The war was finally over! And those who had been spared from death by the enemy were jubilant beyond words.

Millions of multicolored streamers and mountains of confetti rained down on the returning heroes, who had valiantly fought the enemy and won. Friends, family, and fellow citizens danced in the streets to express their own happiness and excitement.

Emotions ran extremely high—unfettered joy, exuberant hope for the future, and unvarnished pride in the victors. But the emotion that ran deepest, causing tears to rush down the faces of moms and dads, grandparents, and even stalwart soldiers—from privates to generals—was *relief*.

The war was over! We were victorious. The soldiers were home. And there was peace at last.

Now that you're home from your spiritual war with God, you must be feeling incredible relief too. With God's help, you've conquered your enemy, the devil. You've been spared from death by Jesus, who acted as your shield in battle. You've been rescued, renewed, and regenerated by God. What amazing feelings of relief and hope and happiness you must be experiencing now. You have personal peace at last!

Still, as a new believer, you probably have many questions. You may be wondering, *Okay, now what? What happens when we become followers of Jesus?* And that's certainly a legitimate question. Here are some things that automatically come with your citizenship in God's kingdom:

You are forgiven! Just think of it! Every sin you've ever committed, without exception—no matter how terrible or heinous—is gone. Jesus took them all onto Himself, and they were nailed to the cross with Him. They are forgiven and forgotten by God. You are pure in His eyes. You are saved.

You are adopted! You have become a child of God! God has adopted you as His own beloved child. You're a member of the Royal Family of heaven. You're a child of the King, and nothing can change that.

The Bible confirms it: "You are all children of God through faith in Christ Jesus" (Galatians 3: 26). This is one reason why it is important for you to become part of a church where Christ is preached, because there you will be with other members of God's family.

You are justified! The moment you were born again, you also received a new nature and were justified in the sight of God. *Justified* means "just-as-if-I'd never sinned." It is God's declaring ungodly people to be perfect in His eyes. God now sees you through the blood of His perfect Son, Christ, which washed away your sins. You are pure and perfect in God's sight.

Christ is living in you! The moment you received Christ as your Lord and Savior, through the Holy Spirit He came to live in your heart. The Bible says, "God decided to let his people know this rich and glorious secret which he has for all people. This secret is Christ himself, who is in you" (Colossians 1:27).

From Old to New. Soldiers who came home from World War II discovered that many changes had happened while they were gone. And they had to go through a period of adjustment as they settled into their new lives. In the same way, you can expect certain changes to take place now that you've been born again. And you will have a period of adjustment as you settle into your new spiritual life with God.

First, because Christ now lives in you, you will have a different attitude toward sin. You will learn to hate sin as God hates it. You will come to detest and abhor it, because God cannot coexist with sin. "We know that those who are God's children [that's you!] do not continue to sin" (1 John 5:18).

Second, you will want to obey God. The Bible says, "We can be sure that we know God if we obey his commands" (1 John 2:3). It will become extremely important to you to do what God says is right and to avoid what God says is wrong. The Bible will become your daily companion.

Third, you will strive to be separated from the world you once followed. The Bible says, "Do not love the world or the things in the world. If you love the world, the love of the Father is not in you" (1 John 2:15). And here's why that's so important: "The world and everything that people want in it are passing away, but the person who does what God wants lives forever" (verse 17). Forever!

Fourth, you'll have a new love for other people. "We know we have left death and have come into life because we love each other. Whoever does not love is still dead" (1 John 3:14). God is love. As His children, we must also "be love" to those around us. You will want to pray for others and help them, instead of ignoring or hating them.

Peace in Your Heart. The Christian life is the best way of living. Don't overlook the advantage that a Christian has both now and for all eternity.

Now! Jesus said, "I came to give life—life in all its fullness" (John 10:10). We don't have to wait until we die to enjoy the blessings of being God's child. He promises that, if we live according to His guidelines for happiness, life will be better now!

Eternally! "God loved the world so much that he gave his one and only Son so that whoever believes in him [that's you!] may not be lost, but have eternal life" (John 3:16).

What a prospect! What a future! What a hope! What a life! I wouldn't change places with the wealthiest and most influential person in the world who didn't know Christ.

I know where I've come from, I know why I'm here, and I know where I'm going . . . and I have personal peace in my heart. His peace overwhelms my soul! In Christ we are at peace even in the midst of problems and pain. The storm may rage, but our hearts are at rest.

We have found personal peace at last![1]

JESUS, YOUR PRINCE OF PEACE

We all long for world peace, but permanent peace among humans eludes the best efforts of world leaders. Peace within the human heart *is* possible, though. Such peace is a telling sign observable in those who have fully surrendered themselves to Jesus. Believers are able to face insecurity and life-threatening possibilities with a deep and abiding peacefulness. Quite simply, the ability to experience the absence of inner conflict, anxiety, and excess stress is rooted in a relationship with the One who is called the Prince of Peace.

The ability to embrace the peace Jesus offers is tied to a good memory. Each of the following memory joggers will prompt us to remember what our Prince of Peace has done in our behalf. These will, in turn, help bring peace to our hearts and minds, no matter what battles are raging within us or around us.

REMEMBER: HE HAS A PLAN

When our lives lack direction, a subconscious battle rages within us. We feel like soldiers on the front lines facing an unknown enemy. Without a purpose or explanation for what is going on at work or at home, our hearts are in combat mode, unable to relax. Our future seems out of control and peace evades us. Jesus is in a position to calm the chaos by reminding us that the future is never uncertain with him. He has a plan for each life. Nothing surprises him. Nothing spins out of his control. Even our own wrong choices can be brought back under his redeeming blood. He can give our lives direction if we are willing to trust him.

As he joined his friends for one last meal the night before his death, Jesus sensed their apprehension. "Let not your heart be troubled; you believe in God, believe also in Me. In My Father's house are many mansions; if it were not so, I would have told you. I go to prepare a place for you. And if I go and prepare a place for you, I will come again and receive you to Myself; that where I am, there you may be also" (John 14:1–3).

Did you notice how Jesus' invitation to be at peace is tied to the fact that he knows what he's doing? Can you visualize Jesus saying those words to you? "Let not your heart be troubled. I'm working out my purpose in your life. I know you aren't always convinced of that. Your restless thoughts and twisted nerves betray your doubt. But your lack of faith does not alter my intentions. Just as I spoke through Jeremiah centuries ago, I say again to you: 'I know what I am planning for you; . . . I have good plans for you, not plans to hurt you. I will give you hope and a good future'" (see Jeremiah 29:11).

But what if those "good plans" are nowhere to be seen? A nineteenth-century London pastor by the name of Charles Spurgeon was willing to admit that Jesus' plans aren't always easy to detect. Spurgeon reminded his flock, "When you can't see his hand, trust his heart." In times when you can't see what Jesus is doing and when you're afraid for the future, trust what you know of him—trust his heart. Remember his promises. Remembering how he has helped you in the past will help you trust in his plan for your future. Give Jesus your anxiety about the future, and be at peace.

REMEMBER: HE IS IN CONTROL

Not only does Jesus have a plan for our lives, he also has the power and the wisdom to work out his plan in a timely and reliable manner.

As you read through the Gospels, try to find Jesus in a hurry. Except for a few boat trips and a brief donkey ride the last week of his life, he walked wherever he went. In spite of the fact that he was often mobbed by needy people reaching out for miracles, he maintained a calm demeanor. Jesus was never in a panic, even if others were. He refused to let the anxiety of others dictate the pace at which his heart beat. Slowly and deliberately he worked his plan. Although his public ministry only lasted a little more than three years, and although he didn't heal every sick person or draw every person in Israel to follow him, he was able to say at the end of his life, "I have finished the work which You have given Me to do" (John 17:4).

Jesus is a portrait of a person who is in full control of the forces around him. When the religious leaders and Roman officials appeared to manipulate the circumstances that culminated in his crucifixion, Jesus was quick to observe, "I give my own life freely" (John 10:18 NCV). On that stormy night on a windblown lake, Jesus demonstrated his control over the forces of nature when he tamed the churning waves.

It's not just stormy weather that Jesus is capable of calming, however. He knows and understands the situations and emotions that rob you of inner peace. Remember: Nothing that is taking place in your life is beyond his control. Like the frightened disciples on the lake that day, call out to Jesus for help. Let him bring peace to the rolling waves that are splashing into your life.

Remember: He Is With You

Personal, inner peace in a world at war is only possible when you believe in the message of Easter Sunday. Once a year Christians gather in lily-filled sanctuaries to greet other believers with "Christ is risen. He is risen, indeed!" But the implications of that ancient affirmation impact every day of the year and every moment of our lives. Jesus defeated death, and he continues to be involved with the world he came to redeem. He is present, although not always seen.

After the crucifixion, and after Jesus' grave was discovered to be empty, Jesus' disciples were locked behind closed doors. Without forewarning, the risen Christ appeared inside the home in which they were gathered. And what were the first words that fell from his lips? "Peace to you!" (John 20:21). And for good reason. Being surprised by his sudden presence must have registered alarm and fear on their faces. It was as if they had seen a ghost. To ease their anxiety, Jesus spoke peace. Jesus' greeting was more than just an antidote to fear, however. When he said "peace," he was reminding them that his presence in their lives removed any reason to be held captive by conflict or gut-wrenching concerns.

Over the next several weeks Jesus kept showing up unannounced. He sat with them and ate with them. When he was with them, he referred to conversations they'd had when he wasn't around as a way of proving he was with them even when they couldn't see him. Although requiring faith to fully digest that truth, such a fact was a source of confidence to them.

He desires that reality to be a source of confidence for you as well. The same person who promised his followers, "I am with you always" (Matthew 28:20) is with you too. Jesus had promised, "I will pray the Father, and He will give you another Helper, that He may abide with you forever—the Spirit of truth, whom the world cannot receive, because it neither sees Him nor knows Him; but you know Him, for He dwells with you and *will be in you*" (John 14:16–17, italics added). The Holy Spirit will grow the fruit of peace in your life (Galatians 5:22).

Allow that reality to wrestle your fear-prone heart from the grip of worry. You can do that by practicing his presence. Jesus is *in you* through his Holy Spirit. Talk to him. Let him in on decisions you are contemplating. Express your nervousness over a coming situation. Be honest about your fears. Picture the Prince of Peace standing right beside you. Let not your heart be troubled. He is with you; let him give you his peace.

SCRIPTURE SELECTIONS

But the fruit of the Spirit is . . . peace . . .

GALATIANS 5:22

The LORD will give strength to His people;
The LORD will bless His people with peace.

PSALM 29:11

I will both lie down in peace, and sleep;
For You alone, O LORD, make me dwell in safety.

PSALM 4:8

For unto us a Child is born,
Unto us a Son is given;
And the government will be upon His shoulder.
And His name will be called
Wonderful, Counselor, Mighty God,
Everlasting Father, Prince of Peace.

ISAIAH 9:6

Peace I leave with you, My peace I give to you; not as the world
gives do I give to you. Let not your heart be troubled, neither let
it be afraid.

JOHN 14:27

These things I have spoken to you, that in Me you may have
peace. In the world you will have tribulation; but be of good
cheer, I have overcome the world.

JOHN 16:33

Therefore, having been justified by faith, we have peace with God through our Lord Jesus Christ, through whom also we have access by faith into this grace in which we stand, and rejoice in hope of the glory of God.

ROMANS 5:1–2

The LORD lift up His countenance upon you,
And give you peace.

NUMBERS 6:26

For He Himself is our peace.

EPHESIANS 2:14

You will keep him in perfect peace,
Whose mind is stayed on You,
Because he trusts in You.

ISAIAH 26:3

And let the peace of God rule in your hearts, to which also you were called in one body; and be thankful.

COLOSSIANS 3:15

Be anxious for nothing, but in everything by prayer and supplication, with thanksgiving, let your requests be made known to God; and the peace of God, which surpasses all understanding, will guard your hearts and minds through Christ Jesus.

PHILIPPIANS 4:6–7

POEMS AND PRAYERS

Peace, Perfect Peace

Peace, perfect peace, in this dark world of sin?
The blood of Jesus whispers peace within.

Peace, perfect peace, by thronging duties pressed?
To do the will of Jesus, this is rest.

Peace, perfect peace, with sorrows surging round?
On Jesus' bosom naught but calm is found.

Peace, perfect peace, with loved ones far away?
In Jesus' keeping we are safe, and they.

Peace, perfect peace, our future all unknown?
Jesus we know, and He is on the throne.

Peace, perfect peace, death shadowing us and ours?
Jesus has vanquished death and all its powers.

It is enough: earth's struggles soon shall cease,
And Jesus call us to Heaven's perfect peace.
—*Edward H. Bickersteth, Jr.*

Jesus, I love to picture you as my Prince of Peace. Thinking of your sovereign power over conflicts that often paralyze me calms my nervous heart. As I picture you on your throne, high and exalted above all things, I can feel my stress evaporate. As I hear you speak "Peace, be still" to the angry waves on the Sea of Galilee, it's as though you are commanding the restless thoughts in my anxious soul to be quiet. Thank you, Jesus, that your presence is all I need to make it through today. Amen.

FOR FURTHER THOUGHT

🙙🙣

1. What situation are you facing today that is causing you fear or concern?
2. What can you do to give that situation over to your Prince of Peace?
3. How do you think the fruit of peace should look in the life of a Christian?
4. Explain what this quote from Charles Spurgeon (quoted above) means to you: "When you can't see his hand, trust his heart."
5. In what ways can you show Jesus that you trust that he has a plan for your life—a good plan, a good future—even if you can't see it right now?

For further reflection on Jesus as your Prince of Peace, listen to "Whisper To Me" on the companion *Jesus* CD.

Jesus, the Lover of My Soul

FEATURING THE WRITING OF DEE BRESTIN AND KATHY TROCCOLI

Jesus entered our world as a living, breathing incarnation of the One who *is* love. "God is love," wrote John the apostle, "and he who abides in love abides in God, and God in him" (1 John 4:16). Wherever Jesus went he courted the hearts of individuals. When he looked at the rich young ruler with love (Mark 10:21), he was looking into the young man's heart and seeing the potential and value of a struggling soul. That Jesus loved his disciples "to the end" (John 13:1) means that he loved his followers with the kind of love that saw past their flaws, their misunderstandings, even their mistakes, and would continue to love them anyway.

Twice during Jesus' ministry, two separate women came to him and anointed his feet with fragrant perfume. The first event is recorded in Luke 7, where "a woman in the city who was a sinner" came to the Pharisee's home where Jesus was having dinner (verse 37). She may have been a prostitute. At some point during his ministry, however, Jesus had touched her heart and she had been overwhelmed by a love she didn't know existed—a clean, pure, eternal love that filled her soul. This was not "love" for money; it was not "love" that lasted only moments. This was forever love. She wanted to thank Jesus for what he had done for her. She discovered where he would be, and she arrived to do what a servant would do for a master—she washed his feet.

She brought an alabaster flask of fragrant oil. The picture Luke gives is poignant:

[She] stood behind Jesus at his feet, crying. She began to wash his feet with her tears, and she dried them with her hair, kissing them many times and rubbing them with the perfume. (Luke 7:38 NCV)

Picture her kneeling at the end of the seat where Jesus was reclining. It was not so unusual for onlookers to hang around at such a dinner. But it was unusual for a woman to approach a group with such a task. No wonder the Pharisee smirked. No wonder he saw this act by this particular woman as a sure sign of Jesus' lack of credentials as a rabbi.

There could not have been a greater contrast between the pious Pharisee across the table and the weeping woman at Jesus' feet. One seeing Jesus as an imposter; the other seeing Jesus as Lover of her soul.

Jesus used the event to teach a powerful lesson about love. He pointed out the woman's act of love and said to the Pharisee:

"Do you see this woman? When I came into your house, you gave me no water for my feet, but she washed my feet with her tears and dried them with her hair. You gave me no kiss of greeting, but she has been kissing my feet since I came in. You did not put oil on my head, but she poured perfume on my feet. I tell you that

*her many sins are forgiven, so she showed great love. But the per-
son who is forgiven only a little will love only a little." (Luke
7:44–47 NCV)*

In other words, only those who understand the depth of their
sin will understand the love Jesus has for them. Like this woman,
they sense Jesus' compassionate, pure, and eternal love, and they
respond with great love themselves.

Jesus looks on us as he did on that woman. His love sees past our
flaws, our misunderstandings, our sins. He knows how desperately
we need him, for nothing else can fill our need for unconditional
love. He reaches out to us at our worst and seeks to make us our
best. What can we do but respond to such love?

The Bible tells the story of another woman who wanted to show
her love for Jesus, and did so in a similar way to the woman in
Luke 7. This story is recorded in John 12. Dee Brestin and Kathy
Troccoli bring that story to life as they envision the love Jesus has
for his people.

READING FROM DEE BRESTIN AND KATHY TROCCOLI

Mary entered the party, a room full of men, carrying her perfume
in an alabaster container. She did what she absolutely had to do.
It didn't matter to her how people would react. All that mattered
to her was Jesus.

Costly perfume was stored in alabaster, which was a kind of
marble. Mary's jar apparently had a long slender neck that could
easily be broken. . . .

Mary's perfume was very valuable indeed. It was worth
approximately a year's wages. But rather than saving it for her
earthly bridegroom, she chose to break the box and pour some of
the perfume on the head of Jesus. Then she sank to her knees and

poured the rest on His feet, wiping them with her long and flow-ing hair. Perhaps she used her hair, rather than a towel, as an indi-cation of her great love for Jesus. . . .

The setting was Bethany, shortly after the raising of Lazarus and six days before the crucifixion of Christ. This incident is often con-fused with an incident in the Book of Luke in which a notably sinful woman, probably a prostitute who had been forgiven, anointed Jesus early in His ministry. It is very important to us that you understand that these were two different incidents and that Mary of Bethany was never a prostitute. The banquet at which Mary of Bethany anointed Jesus was a grateful celebration for the raising of Lazarus. Tradition says the host, Simon the leper, may have been healed by Jesus and was related to the siblings, possibly as their father. If this is true, you can almost imagine the outpouring of gratitude. What joy Simon would have felt at having his only son back!

Matthew, Mark, and John all record this incident, with different details, and only John specifies that the woman was Mary of Bethany. Read carefully the account given by John.

Six days before the Passover, Jesus arrived at Bethany, where Lazarus lived, whom Jesus had raised from the dead. Here a dinner was given in Jesus' honor. Martha served, while Lazarus was among those reclining at the table with him. Then Mary took about a pint of pure nard, an expensive perfume; she poured it on Jesus' feet and wiped his feet with her hair. And the house was filled with the fragrance of the perfume.

But one of his disciples, Judas Iscariot, who was later to betray him, objected, "Why wasn't this perfume sold and the money given to the poor? It was worth a year's wages." He did not say this because he cared about the poor but because he was a thief; as keeper of the money bag, he used to help himself to what was put into it.

"Leave her alone," Jesus replied. "It was intended that she should save this perfume for the day of my burial. You will always have the poor among you, but you will not always have me." (John 12:1–8 NIV)

Have you ever been so overwhelmed with love for Jesus that you simply had to do something? Mary of Bethany loved Jesus so—and now He was also her Prince who had rescued her by raising her precious brother from the dead. . . .

The risk she took was astonishing. Women were supposed to stay in the background. Yet here, with one overwhelming intention, Mary of Bethany boldly enters a house full of men. It doesn't matter to her that she is risking her pride, her reputation, and her dowry—she is ready to abandon all for Jesus. What she does is dramatic, and it causes an enormous stir. The perfume's fragrance filled the whole house and lingered, no doubt, on Jesus through the following holy week, through His crucifixion, and on His body in the grave. Mary of Bethany turned that day into a day that would go down in history. . . .

Mary of Bethany surrendered her pride and her reputation. We are told the disciples rebuked her harshly, but their rebukes simply didn't matter to her. When we are concerned about our own reputation, we are self-conscious and hold in check the loving word that might be spoken, the loving deed that might be done. But those who live an abandoned life seize every opportunity to give encouragement to others, especially those who need it most.

Mary of Bethany surrendered her possessions. Whenever we sing "Take My Life," I (Dee) squirm a little at the line "Take my silver and my gold, not a mite would I withhold." Mother Teresa said, "Give until it hurts."

Mary of Bethany surrendered her time. She sat at His feet, unconcerned about the pressures of life. She knew that if she put

Him first, everything else would fall into place. Often my (Dee's) most precious times with God are in the morning. It's so quiet. I can be all alone with Him. I sometimes hesitate to ask the Lord what His plans are for my day. What will He require of me? It's laughable when I put it into words because I've given Him my life—so why won't I give Him my day?

All of my Christian life I have struggled with breaking the alabaster box of my own agenda. I *know* I have missed God-appointments because I was so focused on what I was doing. Because I am busy writing Christian books, because I am traveling and speaking, it is easy to lose perspective. I can think I am about God's agenda when I may be missing it completely. Isn't that what happened to the priest and the Levite in the parable of the Good Samaritan? They stepped right over the broken and bleeding man, thinking they were serving God. I *know* I have stepped over people in need in my path. They could be seated next to me in the airplane, they could be calling me late at night, or they could be vulnerably telling me about wounds in their life, and I am too preoccupied to feel the severity of their pain. I *know* I have even stepped over the bodies of cherished friends, my own children, my own grandchildren, and my precious elderly parents. How depraved I am. How in need of God's grace. Jesus *never* saw people as interruptions. His only focus was His Father's will, His Father's agenda. He *truly,* as James tells us to do, saw interruptions as friends.

Why do I hold on to my own agenda so tightly? Because I forget that my life must be about Jesus, and not centered around me. The selfish Dee is still kicking. I pray she'll learn how to die.

And so I continually ask God to change my heart. Kathy has been such a model for me, speaking the truth to me when she sees me hesitate to be merciful.

Just this week someone called wanting to chat. Often I am

reserved with her, because her chats can become lengthy. But this time I didn't shut up my compassions. His Spirit reminded me to be the love of Jesus to her. At the end of the phone call, she said, "This meant so much to me, Dee. I always feel like you are so busy—but I must have caught you at a good time." (I hung up and wept. And then, *yes,* I sensed *His* pleasure.)

Each time I break the alabaster box of my own agenda at His feet, the fragrance fills the room, bringing joy to weary faces, and surrounding me, enveloping me with peace and an inextinguishable joy.

In the last two years, I've been praying daily that I would love Jesus more. More growth has occurred in the last two years than in any other period in my life. Why? It's simple, really. As His love wells up in me, it is like the sap that rises in the spring, pushing off those ugly stubborn leaves that have clung tenaciously to the branches all winter. It's exciting when I see the leaves fall, because when they do, I know I'm allowing room for new life. . . .

One of my (Kathy's) alabaster boxes has been the desire for success. My mother always said, "My daughter is going to be somebody." I have a picture of me in the fifth-grade choir where the mothers were obviously told to dress their kids in white shirts and dark skirts or pants. But my mother dressed me in a bright red jumper. I smile and shake my head every time I look at it. My mother was going to make sure I stood out.

When I first moved to Nashville in my twenties, my family had such high hopes and dreams for me. I was managed by the same men who managed Amy Grant, and that started the whole process of God humbling me. When I was in Long Island, I was the big fish in the small pond, and now I was watching Nashville's princess walk through my dreams. I started working in a little Christian bookstore, and my family couldn't understand why things weren't happening. I did get out my first recording,

Stubborn Love, in 1982. I'm not saying I didn't have a certain amount of success at that time, because I did. But it didn't quite happen the way I thought it was going to. All these years later, I realize that God was protecting me from having too much too soon. I realize now that God was developing a holy brokenness and humility in me that could not have happened had I not lived through that season in my life. I've often hung on to Mother Teresa's words: "Faithfulness, not success." God is sovereign. And whether or not I ever sing another note, I am God's Beloved. He desires relationship with me. That is the most important thing.

At this time in my life, God is allowing me to step into arenas where I am speaking and singing to thousands of women. My spirit often says, "Ahhhh." The years of feeling like things should be happening in a certain way (ways I had imagined), the years of feeling forgotten by God, feeling like a stepchild, have prepared me for such a time as this. He's patiently loved me and taught me and revealed Himself to me. And that is how I'm able to speak to women boldly and confidently about Jesus. Whether I'm addressing eating disorders, self-esteem, death, bitterness toward an ex-husband, an abortion, or the hundred other things women face every day of their lives, the solution is the same. The answer is the same. We must know God. We must be honest with Him. We must be willing to pick up the cross He offers us, knowing there will always be a resurrection. Always.

Do Dee and I still get frustrated? Do we still question God? Do I still have days when lifting my head from the pillow feels like an impossible chore? Absolutely. We're trapped in these bodies and we will deal with these things until we see Him face to face. Until then, we must cling desperately to the One who is crazy about us, to the One who has promised us wholeness, to the One who has promised to never let us go. . . .

My favorite time of year is autumn. Leaves turning, it's nature's fashion show. Armani, Calvin Klein, and Versace wish they could look this good! Yet what penetrates my heart is that amidst this lavish exhibit, there is a complete dying process going on. Every leaf that boldly expresses its splendor will eventually fall to the ground. Dry and barren. Its beauty seemingly gone forever. Until spring . . . new buds, new life, a new creation.

When we die to ourselves, when we break our alabaster box, it is an act of faith—that from death will come life. Do we believe there will be a resurrection? So often we don't believe it. We don't want to die to ourselves because we don't believe God will do His part. But He will.

He certainly did with Mary of Bethany. What she did turned out to be an enormous blessing, not just for Jesus, but for her, and for generations to come.

Did Mary know what was going to happen as a result of her sacrifice? Jesus said that Mary poured perfume on Him to prepare His body for burial. Did she know Jesus was going to be crucified? Did she intend for her perfume to anoint Him for His burial? Some are absolutely convinced she understood; others are just as convinced she did not. Read the account Mark gives:

> While he was in Bethany, reclining at the table in the home of a man known as Simon the Leper, a woman came with an alabaster jar of very expensive perfume, made of pure nard. She broke the jar and poured the perfume on his head.
>
> Some of those present were saying indignantly to one another "Why this waste of perfume? It could have been sold for more than a year's wages and the money given to the poor." And they rebuked her harshly.
>
> "Leave her alone," said Jesus. "Why are you bothering her? She has done a beautiful thing to me. The poor you will always have with you, and you can help them any time you

want. But you will not always have me. She did what she
could. She poured perfume on my body beforehand to pre-
pare for my burial. I tell you the truth, wherever the gospel
is preached throughout the world, what she has done will
also be told, in memory of her." (Mark 14:3–9 NIV)

Perhaps Mary was simply led of the Holy Spirit but didn't know how meaningful her act was going to be. Perhaps she knew He was going to die but didn't know how soon or that she was actually preparing His body for burial. Yet Christ turns and canonizes her on the spot, astonishing all in the room. . . .

I (Dee) think Mary may have understood that Jesus was going to die very soon and may even have understood that she was anointing Him for His burial. It seems to me that Jesus implied she understood. I have often seen that those who sit at the feet of Jesus, listening to Him intently, are more apt to see things that fly completely over the heads of others.

Repeatedly in Scripture the Lord lets us know that those who earnestly desire to know Him, to see Him, and to understand Him will. He spoke in riddles and parables to hide things from those who were not welcoming Him but was eager to reveal Himself to those with seeking hearts. Do you remember how the Lord said, "Shall I hide from Abraham what I am about to do?" (Genesis 18:17)? The Lord chose not to hide the truth from Abraham, the friend of God. I think it is possible that the Lord chose also not to hide the truth from Mary of Bethany because she too was truly His friend and earnestly desired to understand and obey. . . .

For some time Jesus had been telling His followers that He was going to Jerusalem to die, and they'd look at Him with glazed eyes and say, "Huh?" But I think it is at least possible that Mary of Bethany understood, because she loved Him so much and heartily wanted to understand Him. The psalmist tells us the

Lord confides in those who worship Him (based on Psalm 25:14a AMP).

When I read a commentary that says, "Of course Mary didn't understand," I think, *Why do you say "of course"?* Mary had seen Jesus raise her brother from the dead. She had seen Him do the impossible. She also could see that all were not pleased. Did she hear that some were plotting to take the life of Jesus and of Lazarus? I think she may very well have seen the thunderclouds rolling in, the storm on the horizon, and was quite purposeful in what she did.

But perhaps it is simply my pride as a woman that relishes the irony that a woman, considered to be the inferior gender in that culture (but not by Jesus), gleaned what all the men had missed.

But whether Mary of Bethany understood or not, she certainly provides a sharp relief to the actions and attitudes around her: an act of love in the midst of hate, for the plotting against Jesus immediately precedes the anointing, and the betrayal immediately follows it. Likewise, Mary is a contrast to the bumbling disciples, who are quite confident that they are right to harshly rebuke her. In the midst of pride and greed she comes, humbly breaking her precious alabaster box and wiping His feet with her unbound hair.

In obeying the prompting of the Spirit, she left a legacy. In fact, as Jesus prophesied, wherever the gospel is preached throughout the world, what Mary of Bethany did is told, in memory of her. She is unforgettable.

And if we die to ourselves, we can be unforgettable too.[1]

JESUS, LOVER OF YOUR SOUL

Jesus loves us. When we come to Jesus, we are simply responding to his love. It does not matter that we feel undeserving of his love, that we cannot repay it, or that we cannot understand it. All

Jesus wants is for us to accept it. Like both women in the stories above, we can bring our most precious possessions—ourselves and whatever we hold in our "alabaster jars"—and lovingly offer them to Jesus.

CREATED TO LOVE

Every person who has ever lived has dreamed of being held and affirmed, comforted, and celebrated. It's a universal desire. Infants need love that is completely unconditional—late-night feedings and all. As we grow, we seek such love from our families; we long to be loved for who we are. Many people then seek that lifetime spouse with whom to live, love, and grow old. That's just the way we were created.

Before the world surrendered its paradise status, the roots of love reached deep into the earth and pushed their way into human hearts. In a verdant garden lush with leafy shrubs and flowering trees, a lonely man longed for more than the beauty of creation. His world was seemingly perfect, yet something was lacking. The Creator saw the solitary creature's predicament. The One who had proclaimed His creative endeavor in the cosmos "good" and his prototype human "very good" now verbalized a contrary sentiment: "It is not good for the man to be alone" (Genesis 2:18 NCV).

In response to the hunger of the man's heart, God created a woman. In the gift of Eve, God gave Adam a lover of his soul. And from that time on, a craving for committed companionship and mutual affection has been passed on to every descendant of that first couple.

We were born with a longing to be loved. That desire obviously motivates our movement toward marriage. But it's also just as obvious that our needs for love, acceptance, and forgiveness cannot be completely fulfilled in any human relationship. The loneliness God originally saw in Adam was only partially assuaged by Eve. Human companions fail us or leave us through divorce or death. God knew what Adam eventually discovered: The hunger for love in every human's heart can only be completely satisfied by an intimacy with God himself.

LET GOD LOVE YOU

For some, the thought of "intimacy" with Jesus makes them uncomfortable. They would prefer not to deal with the kind of love that causes them to fall on their knees in front of the "Pharisees" in their lives. They'd prefer not to break their alabaster jars in thanksgiving for his love for them. They'd rather have love from a distance. Jesus as Friend is fine; Jesus as Lover of their souls . . . well, they're not so sure they're ready for that, or that they even want it.

Before he became chaplain of the U.S. Senate, Lloyd John Ogilvie was the pastor of the influential First Presbyterian Church of Hollywood and host of a weekly television program called *Let God Love You.* The title of that broadcast was more than just a catchy phrase. It suggested that those who would benefit from the passionate love of Jesus must place themselves in a position to receive it. They must willingly allow the Lord to draw near.

To find true, eternal, unconditional love—perfect love—go to the source of love, the Lover of your soul. Nothing and no one else will do. If you're fortunate, some human loves in your life will come close, but that only whets your desire to understand and experience perfect love. If you've had the pain of a broken heart, remember that Jesus is far different from those who have caused your pain. It may not be easy, but if you are willing to open your heart once again, he will love you as no human being ever has.

So let him draw near to you. You can best do that by drawing near to him. Just as you set aside time to be with the special people in your life, set aside time to be with God. Make him a priority.

Spend quiet time alone with him. Open his Word and read it as a love letter to you. Talk to him—about everything. Open your heart. Then listen. "Draw near to God and He will draw near to you" (James 4:8). Know that the Lover of your soul is faithful to do all that he says he will do. "Draw near with a true heart in full assurance of faith, . . . hold fast the confession of our hope without wavering, for He who promised is faithful" (Hebrews 10:22–23).

FOR MEN ONLY

Men do not relate as easily as women to the image of Christ as Lover of their souls. But if you are a man, the image need not be lost on you.

Too many men reach midlife having achieved a degree of success in the place where they work but admitting to unfinished business in the place where their emotions dwell. Men who grew up in a culture where feelings were not freely shared and affection was viewed as unmanly offered confusing signals to their sons. A lack of tangible love contributed to a lack of self-esteem. Acceptance too often was viewed as conditional, and the longing to know they were unique and special went unquenched.

If that person is you, the father's love you never knew is found in the Father who loves your soul. But to experience that firsthand (and to the degree God desires), you may need to experience that love for yourself tangibly. Consider connecting with two or three other men—perhaps from your Sunday school class or other small group. Share your personal stories about growing up. Talk about how your father expressed (or didn't express) love. Verbalize your longings for acceptance and belonging. Pray for each other.

YOU ARE LOVED

Jesus loves you, so don't hold him at arm's length or you will miss out on the greatest love possible. Allow yourself to experience his love.

"But how?" you may ask. "I'm not lovable, sometimes not even likable. I'm not beautiful. I'm so flawed, so sinful, so impure. How can he possibly love me?" Or perhaps you've been hurt badly. Your heart is bruised and bandaged. You're feeling that you're never going to open yourself to love again. It hurts far too much.

To those who feel undeserving of such love, the Bible promises that you don't need to *deserve* it, and you couldn't if you tried. Jesus loved you before you loved him. Paul wrote, "But God shows his great love for us in this way: Christ died for us while we were still sinners" (Romans 5:8 NCV).

To those who don't want to be hurt anymore, to those who say with the psalmist, "I am weary with my crying; my throat is dry; my eyes fail while I wait for my God" (Psalm 69:3), God says, "I have loved you with an everlasting love" (Jeremiah 31:3). He promises a day in the future when he will wipe away every tear from your eyes (Revelation 21:4).

Jesus understood how much God loves us: "I will be in them and you will be in me so that they will be completely one. Then the world will know that you sent me and that you loved them just as much as you loved me" (John 17:23 NCV).

You see, you don't have to *do* anything to be loved by Jesus. He already loves you. You simply need to receive his love. A hymn writer put it this way:

> *O Love that wilt not let me go,*
> *I rest my weary soul in thee;*
> *I give thee back the life I owe,*
> *That in thine ocean depths its flow*
> *May richer, fuller be.*
> —*"O Love That Wilt Not Let Me Go," George Matheson (1882)*

SCRIPTURE SELECTIONS

I am my beloved's,
And his desire is toward me.

SONG OF SOLOMON 7:10

The LORD has appeared of old to me, saying:
"Yes, I have loved you with an everlasting love;
Therefore with lovingkindness I have drawn you."

JEREMIAH 31:3

The LORD your God in your midst,
The Mighty One, will save;
He will rejoice over you with gladness,
He will quiet you with His love,
He will rejoice over you with singing.

ZEPHANIAH 3:17

For God so loved the world that He gave His only begotten Son,
that whoever believes in Him should not perish but have ever-
lasting life.

JOHN 3:16

As the Father loved Me, I also have loved you; abide in My love.
If you keep My commandments, you will abide in My love, just
as I have kept My Father's commandments and abide in His
love. . . . Greater love has no one than this, than to lay down
one's life for his friends.

JOHN 15:9, 10, 13

But God demonstrates His own love toward us, in that while we were still sinners, Christ died for us.

ROMANS 5:8

For I am persuaded that neither death nor life, nor angels nor principalities nor powers, nor things present nor things to come, nor height nor depth, nor any other created thing, shall be able to separate us from the love of God which is in Christ Jesus our Lord.

ROMANS 8:38–39

I have been crucified with Christ; it is no longer I who live, but Christ lives in me; and the life which I now live in the flesh I live by faith in the Son of God, who loved me and gave Himself for me.

GALATIANS 2:20

Behold what manner of love the Father has bestowed on us, that we should be called children of God! Therefore the world does not know us, because it did not know Him.

1 JOHN 3:1

By this we know love, because He laid down His life for us. And we also ought to lay down our lives for the brethren.

1 JOHN 3:16

He who does not love does not know God, for God is love. In this the love of God was manifested toward us, that God has sent His only begotten Son into the world, that we might live through Him. In this is love, not that we loved God, but that He loved us and sent His Son to be the propitiation for our sins.

1 JOHN 4:8–10

POEMS AND PRAYERS

ɷ

Love Divine, All Loves Excelling

Love divine, all loves excelling,
Joy of heaven to earth come down;
Fix in us thy humble dwelling;
All thy faithful mercies crown!
Jesus, Thou art all compassion,
Pure unbounded love Thou art;
Visit us with Thy salvation;
Enter every trembling heart.

Breathe, O breathe Thy loving Spirit,
Into every troubled breast!
Let us all in Thee inherit;
Let us find that second rest.
Take away our bent to sinning;
Alpha and Omega be;
End of faith, as its Beginning,
Set our hearts at liberty.

Come, Almighty to deliver,
Let us all Thy life receive;
Suddenly return and never,
Never more Thy temples leave.
Thee we would be always blessing,
Serve Thee as Thy hosts above,
Pray and praise Thee without ceasing,
Glory in Thy perfect love.

Finish, then, Thy new creation;
Pure and spotless let us be.
Let us see Thy great salvation
Perfectly restored in Thee;
Changed from glory into glory,
Till in heaven we take our place,
Till we cast our crowns before Thee,
Lost in wonder, love, and praise.
—*Charles Wesley (1747)*

Jesus, thank you for loving me. Help me to learn more each day about this love relationship. Help me to make you a priority, seeking to spend quiet time with you each day—talking, listening, learning. Help me to accept your love—knowing I am unworthy, yet grateful that you have made me worthy to be called your own. I love you, dear Jesus. I love you.

FOR FURTHER THOUGHT

1. How does it make you feel to know that Jesus is the Lover of your soul?
2. How do you react to a love that will not let you go?
3. Describe a time when you felt Jesus' love for you.
4. How are you letting Jesus love you?
5. In what ways are you showing Jesus that you love him?

For further reflection on Jesus as Lover of my soul, listen to "In the Garden/There Is None Like You" on the companion *Jesus* CD.

Jesus, the Savior

FEATURING THE WRITING OF ANNE GRAHAM LOTZ

J esus saves."

Perhaps you've seen the phrase on a bumper sticker or a billboard as you traveled along the highway. You read the words and then continued on your way, yet the phrase might have lingered in your mind, perhaps with a question: "Jesus saves . . . Whom does he save? And from what?"

Those are fair questions. When we think of someone being saved, we usually picture a rescue of some sort. Perhaps we envision a lifeguard saving a swimmer from drowning or a fireman saving a person from a burning building. A person in danger escaped harm or death because someone stepped in to save him or her. Is that what we mean when we say, "Jesus saves"?

Absolutely.

The Bible gives us the story, for that is what the Bible is about from beginning to end—Jesus saves. The Bible describes a perfect creation marred by sin. Sin sent mankind into a downward spiral from which we can never recover on our own, for sin is part of our

very nature. All we need to do is look briefly into our own thoughts
and hearts to discover that sin is there whether we like it or not, no
matter how hard we may try to avoid it.

And therein lies the problem. God is holy; we are filled with sin.
Like oil and water, sin and holiness just don't mix. We can never
have a relationship with God. In fact, we're slated for judgment and
death. The Bible says, "The wages of sin is death" (Romans 6:23).

But God wanted more for us. Besides being perfectly holy, God
is also love. He desired to have a relationship with the people he
created. He wanted us to be with him forever. Yet, God is also perfectly just. He could not turn a blind eye to our sin. Something had
to be done; punishment had to be given so justice could be served.

Enter Jesus.

Perfect man. Perfect God. Perfect sacrifice. He came specifically
to take upon himself the punishment for our sins. When he died
on the cross, God considered it payment in full for every sin across
time. The prophet Isaiah wrote of him, "He was wounded for our
transgressions, He was bruised for our iniquities; the chastisement
for our peace was upon Him, and by His stripes we are healed"
(Isaiah 53:5).

Those very words provide the first visual on the screen at Mel
Gibson's movie *The Passion of the Christ*. Those words explain that
the film's realistic portrayal of Jesus' last days is not some horror
story without a point. That suffering was for *us*. He was bruised for
our iniquities. He was nailed to that awful cross for *our* sins. That
was the payment God required. That was the payment God paid
on our behalf.

The relentless torture of the movie makes us wince. And it
should. We watch as Jesus is bludgeoned, beaten, and bloodied. Yet
Jesus keeps going. Why? Because he knows that only he can
accomplish the task before him. Only he can be the sacrifice that
will pay for sin.

Jesus saves. He saves us from the punishment of death our sins deserve. He saves us so that we can have a personal and eternal relationship with God.

In her book *Just Give Me Jesus*, Anne Graham Lotz draws a vivid picture of Jesus as the Savior. Starting with the system of animal sacrifice in the Old Testament, she describes why Jesus had to die, how he died, and what his death accomplished for all who come to him to save them.

READING FROM ANNE GRAHAM LOTZ

In the Old Testament, when a person sinned, he was required to take the very best, blue-ribbon lamb he could find, one without any spots or blemishes, to the priest at the temple. There, in front of the priest, the sinner would grasp the lamb with both hands and confess his sin. His guilt was transferred to the lamb as though it had traveled through his arms and hands to the terrified little creature. The priest would then hand the sinner a knife, and the sinner would kill the lamb so that it was obvious the lamb had died as a result of the sinner's action. Then the priest would take the blood of the lamb and sprinkle it on the altar to make atonement for the man's sin.

Throughout the years, fountains of blood and rivers of blood and oceans of blood flowed from the temple altar as God's children sought His forgiveness for their sin. Yet when they walked away from such a sacrifice, their hearts must have remained heavy as the burden of guilt clung like river slime to their souls. The writer to the Hebrews put it bluntly: "It is impossible for the blood of bulls and goats [and lambs] to take away sins" (Hebrews 10:4 NIV). So why the sacrificial slaughter?

The entire bloody ritual was like an IOU note that bought the sinner temporary atonement until a perfect sacrifice would come and pay it off. And the perfect Sacrifice did come.

One day, as John the Baptist was standing beside the River Jordan, a rather ordinary-looking man walked past. John recognized Him as his cousin, Jesus of Nazareth. But John didn't call Him by His given name. Instead, John pointed and identified Him as "the Lamb of God, who takes away the sin of the world!" (John 1:29 NIV). John was making the most remarkable announcement since the angels had heralded the birth of the Baby in Bethlehem. With razorlike perception, he recognized that Jesus Himself would be the perfect Lamb who would pay off all those IOU notes with the sacrifice of Himself.

The pervasive misconception today is that since Jesus died as a sacrifice for the sins of the world, then we are all automatically forgiven. But we overlook the vital truth that we must grasp the Lamb with our hands of faith and confess our sins. We then must acknowledge that He was slain for our sins as surely as if we had plunged the knife into His heart. At that moment, the Lamb becomes our High Priest and offers His own blood on the altar of the cross on our behalf. And, wonder of wonders! God accepts the sacrifice and we are forgiven! Our guilt is atoned for! We are made right in God's sight! Jesus, the Lamb of God, makes sin forgivable for everyone!

Following His six trials, Jesus was turned over to the Roman soldiers, who led Him to the place called Calvary for crucifixion. Jesus had been on His feet for nine hours during which time He had been manhandled, spit upon, slapped, flogged, and dragged from place to place. His back was already a mangled, bloody mess from the scourging when the soldiers roughly placed a cross on it, demanding that He carry His own means of execution through the streets of Jerusalem. . . .

As Jesus struggled to make His way through the narrow streets crowded with the throngs of pilgrims who had come to celebrate the Feast of the Passover, He heard not only cheers and jeers, but also tears. He did not rebuke the mockery, but He did rebuke the misery of a large group of women who wept and wailed for Him. He actually stopped on His way to Calvary and admonished, "Daughters of Jerusalem, do not weep for me; weep for yourselves and for your children" because of the judgment of God that would fall on them because of that day (Luke 23:28 NIV). Jesus flatly rejected their sympathy and pity.

As we meditate on the sacrifice of the Lamb of God, we need to beware of feeling sorry for Him. Instead, our hearts should be crushed from the weight of sorrow for our own sin that cost Him His life—sin that provokes the judgment of God on us unless we confess it and repent of it.

Jesus was not a helpless victim of Roman cruelty or religious jealousy or general apathy. He was the Lamb of God who was deliberately sacrificed for the sin of the world. Yet He was as human as He was divine, and in His humanity He suffered. . . .

Jesus, in His humanity, knew what the guilt and shame of hatred, of murder, of rape, of stealing, of lying feels like, as well as every other sin, big or small, that's ever been thought of or committed. As He hung on the cross, stripped of His own robe of righteousness, He was exposed, spiritually naked in our sins with no hiding place from His Father's penetrating gaze of searing holiness.

Have you ever been caught doing something you shouldn't have? Caught breaking the speed limit? Caught sneaking a piece of cake on your diet? Caught in a lie? Caught in gossip? Do you remember the guilty feeling of shame? That's only a glimmer of the emotional trauma Jesus experienced as He was "caught" in your sins and mine.

Yet because Jesus was stripped "naked," you and I can be clothed! The Bible tells us that all of our righteousness, including the very best things we ever do, are so permeated with sin and selfishness that they are like filthy rags in God's sight. But at the cross, Jesus gave us His perfect, spotless robe of righteousness and took our filthy garments of sin in exchange. On Judgment Day, you and I will be dressed in His righteousness before God because He wore the filthy garments of our sin.

When Jesus was stripped of His physical clothes, the execution squad of soldiers divided what little He had between them—His belt, sandals, and other things. But when it came to His beautifully woven inner garment, they decided that instead of tearing it into four pieces, they would gamble for it. So while Jesus hung slightly above them, groaning in excruciating pain, fighting for His breath, they callously ignored Him and tossed the dice (John 19:23–24). Their ribald laughter and the clatter of the dice as they were thrown made a sharp contrast to His pain-wracked sobs so near by.

People today still toss the dice for the robe of His righteousness. While coldly ignoring His death on the cross, they gamble for His "robe" by betting their eternal lives on the chance that they can earn acceptance with God through their religiosity, or their sincerity, or their morality, or their philanthropy. They "bet" that

if they read their Bibles every day,

if they just do more good works than bad works,

if they keep the Ten Commandments,

if they go to church regularly,

if they're good,

then they have a "chance" to please God and get to heaven— they have a chance to get His "robe." But His "robe" cannot be gambled for, bought, earned, deserved, inherited, given, bartered, or stolen.

The only way to obtain it is to exchange it for your own filthy shreds of righteousness at the cross. His robe is free, not because it is cheap, but because it is priceless. The guilt of your sin and mine has been removed because it was placed on Him, and His righteousness was placed on us! Praise God! What an exchange!

Jesus hung on the cross for three hours, wracked with white-hot physical pain, tortured mentally and emotionally by the taunting and the tempting and the trauma, crushed by the weight of guilt and shame and sin that was ours but became His. Suddenly, the birds stopped chirping, the vultures stopped circling, the breeze stopped blowing, and everything became deathly still as darkness—pitch-black darkness—descended. The cries that could be heard were no longer just coming from the victims on the crosses but from the bystanders as they cowered, then fled in panic like rats scurrying to leave a sinking ship. Even the hardened soldiers must have shuddered at the supernatural power and anger that permeated the atmosphere.

As terrified people looked up, searching the sky, there were no clouds to block the sun. There was no eclipse. The sun was nowhere to be seen! Where it had been was just blackness! Why? Why was the world plunged into what seemed like the very pit of hell?

The eerie darkness that descended was not just nature feeling sorry for the Creator who was nailed to the altar of the cross. It was the very judgment of God for your sins and mine that was poured out on Jesus! What He went through is beyond our ability to imagine or describe. I do know that because Jesus is God, as well as Man, He may have entered an eternal state of time as He hung on the cross.

God created time for your benefit and mine—sixty-second minutes and sixty-minute hours and twenty-four-hour days were set in motion by the tides and the rotation of the earth on its axis. But God does not live by our time clocks. He transcends time. That's why Peter said that one day with the Lord is as a thousand years, and a thousand years is as a day. That's why it may be that He created the world in six days on our time clocks, but thousands of years (even millions of years?) on His time clock. Could it be that although Jesus hung on the cross for six hours according to our time clock, it was actually an eternity of time on His clock? Did Jesus live through an eternity of God's judgment for your sin and my sin as He hung there on the cross? We won't know the answer until we get to heaven, but we do know that He took God's judgment for us. He paid the price in full, and He paid for it with His life.

In the Old Testament, Abraham's faith was tested when God told him to take his son, his only son, the son he loved, and offer him as a sacrifice. And Abraham did. Abraham bound Isaac to the altar and raised his knife to slay him in strict obedience to God's word. Just before the gleaming knife plunged down, God leaned out of heaven and urgently commanded, "Abraham! Abraham! . . . Do not lay a hand on the boy," and Isaac's life was spared! Abraham looked around; caught in the thicket nearby was a ram. After cutting Isaac loose, Abraham took the ram and offered it on the altar. And I wonder, did Isaac embrace the ram with tears streaming down his cheeks, knowing it was a substitute that would die in his place?

As God's Son, God's only Son, the Son He loved, hung on the cross, the knife of God's fierce wrath against sin was lifted, and there was no one to stay the Father's hand. Instead, "He . . . did not spare his own Son, but gave him up for us all" (Romans 8:32 NIV). Jesus was God's Lamb and our Substitute who endured the full force of God's wrath for your sins and mine when He was bound on the altar in our place.

At midafternoon, the silent darkness was pierced with a heart-wrenching cry that would have sent chills down even the stiffest backs. It came from the cracked lips and the crushed heart of God's Son as His tortured body and fevered mind were pushed to the outer limits of endurance. "My God, my God, why have you forsaken me?" (Matthew 27:46 NIV). For the first time in eternity, the Father and Son were actually separated. They were separated by all of your sins and my sins, which came between Them. And

Jesus, suffocating physically, was smothered spiritually by a blanket of loneliness such as He had never known.

Even when Jesus had been alone in a crowd, or alone on a mountainside, or alone on the lake, or alone in a boat, or alone in a room, He had never truly been alone! His Father had always been with Him. He and His Father were so close they were One. To be separated was a spiritual death that was worse than a living nightmare. It was hell!

No one on this side of hell will ever know the loneliness Jesus endured on the cross—in your place and mine. When we claim the Lamb as our own sacrifice for sin, we will never be separated from God, because Jesus was. Praise His dear Name! He is still Emmanuel—God with us. The sacrifice of the Lamb is absolutely sufficient in itself to take away our sin and reconcile us to God.

The blood of Jesus is sufficient for the forgiveness of any and all sins because the Cross was two thousand years ago and all of our sins were still to come. Therefore, all of our sins, whether we committed them yesterday or today or have yet to commit them tomorrow, are covered by His blood—past sins, present sins, future sins, big sins, small sins, or medium-size sins—it makes no difference. . . .

Praise God for the blood of Jesus that is sufficient to cover all of our sins! All of them! . . . They are all under the blood of Jesus, and we are free just to enjoy our forgiveness! We will never be held accountable for the guilt of our sins because Jesus has taken the punishment for us.

This lesson was brought home to me when a thunderstorm broke one Wednesday morning, deluging everything and everyone with rain as I arrived at the church to teach my weekly Bible class. In just a few moments, the parking lot became a fast-flowing two-inch-deep river, and the steps to the church looked like a multitiered waterfall. As I stood in the narthex looking through the sheets of wind-swept rain, I could see a stream of cars organizing itself into neat rows, their headlights sparkling in the raindrops. As I continued to watch, I noticed one woman make a mad dash from her car to the church, umbrella still tightly folded in her hand. She burst through the door, hair askew, makeup smeared, and clothes dripping with water. I sprang to help her, taking her Bible and notebook while she began to shake herself off. I couldn't help but ask with some astonishment, "You have an umbrella. Why didn't you put it up?"

She laughingly replied, "I thought it was just too much trouble."

The rain that fell on everyone and everything that morning is like the wrath of God that falls on all of us because we have all sinned. It is inevitable that sooner or later we will come under His wrath and get "wet." But God has given us an "umbrella" in the blood of Jesus. When we "put it up" by claiming His death for our sins, the umbrella of His blood covers us. God's wrath still falls on our sins, but now our sins are on Jesus; under the umbrella of His blood, we stay dry, and we are saved from the rain of God's wrath.

There is only one umbrella that is sufficient to save us or keep us dry in the midst of the storm of God's wrath. God gave you and me the umbrella when He sent Jesus to the cross to shed His blood for you. Are you still clutching it tightly, unopened? Why? Do you think it's just too much trouble to confess your sins, to repent, to claim Jesus as your Savior and surrender your life to Him as Lord? *Please! Go to the trouble!* The umbrella of the blood of Jesus is absolutely sufficient to save you from the rain of God's wrath, but you have to deliberately, consciously, personally put it up! *Put it up!*

As Jesus cried out from the cross, we can hear Him still clinging by faith to whom He knew His beloved Father to be—*My God.* Even as the sound left His lips, the darkness lifted and He called out hoarsely, "I am thirsty" (John 19:28 NIV). He wasn't asking for a sedative, but something to moisten His swollen tongue and cracked lips. He had something He wanted to say, and He wanted to say it so the angels in heaven would hear it, and the demons in hell would hear it, and people throughout the ages would hear it, and you would hear it, and I would hear it. One of the soldiers standing guard soaked a sponge in wine vinegar, "put the sponge on a stalk of the hyssop plant, and lifted it to Jesus' lips" (John 19:29 NIV).

After nine hours of standing on His feet, after being scourged, slapped, and manhandled, after six hours of hanging on the cross, the average person would have barely had enough life and breath left to even whisper. But Jesus, the Lamb of God, with life still fully flowing through His body, shouted out in a clear, ringing, triumphant voice, "It is finished" (John 19:30 NIV). The price for our redemption had been paid! The sacrifice for our sin had been made!

Sin was forgiven! Guilt was atoned for! Eternal life was now offered! Heaven has been opened! It is finished!

You don't have to do more good works than bad works.

You don't have to go to church every time the door opens.

You don't have to count beads.

You don't have to climb the stairs to some statue.

You don't have to lie on a bed of nails.

You don't have to be religious.

You don't even have to be good!

It is finished! Sin is forgivable for everyone! The price has been paid! Jesus paid it all!

Hallelujah!
Hallelujah!
HALLELUJAH!
HALLELUJAH!

As the clarion shout of victory still echoed in the air, Jesus irrevocably handed His life to His Father as He uttered His last words in a ringing declaration of faith: "Father, into your hands I commit my spirit" (Luke 23:46 NIV). Then He bowed His head and deliberately refused to take the next breath. He just refused to push up. The One who is the Lord of life,

the Resurrection and the Life,

the Creator of life,

the Source of all life,

gave His life for you and me!

And the blood of the Lamb that was shed on the altar of the cross that day ran down the wooden beam, down a hill called Calvary, and down through the years until it reaches us, where it has become a river that is deep enough to bathe in. Isn't it time you plunged in and took a bath? If you agree, pray this simple prayer by faith:

Dear God,

I choose to grasp the Lamb with my hands of faith and confess to You the hardness of my heart, the meanness of my thoughts, the coldness of my spirit, and the sinfulness of my life. I'm so sorry. I know it was for me—and because of me—that Jesus died. Please forgive me of all of my sins—big sins, medium sins, and small sins; past sins, present sins, and future sins. I choose deliberately to put up my umbrella right now. And I want to exchange my filthy garments for His spotless robe.

Thank You for the cleansing fountain of the blood of Jesus that washes me white as snow. I know even now that I am clean and forgiven and "dressed" for heaven.

Thank You! Thank You! Thank You for just giving me Jesus![1]

JESUS, YOUR SAVIOR

Of the countless millions who have seen *The Passion of the Christ*, most have been moved by the images—many to tears. People can't help but respond emotionally to that kind of brutality and to that kind of love. As they watched Jesus being tortured, many no doubt found themselves wondering how they would have reacted if they had been there. As they watched Mary wince at her son's suffering, they probably put themselves in her place, feeling the pulse of her broken heart and her unimaginable agony.

But simply being moved with pity by the suffering of a first-century rabbi falls short of what Jesus intended his death to accomplish. He wanted to move us beyond pity to a personal relationship with him that he made possible by his death. By his own admission, Jesus willingly submitted to inhumane torture and death in order to pay a ransom that would free us from spiritual captivity. He told his followers: "I am the good shepherd. The good shepherd gives His life for the sheep" (John 10:11), and "Greater love has no one than this, than to lay down one's life for his friends" (John 15:13).

In other words, Jesus the Savior doesn't want us to linger at the foot of the cross. His desire is that we walk away from that bloody scene, convinced that the sacrifice that was accomplished on that stormy Friday afternoon two centuries ago is deeply personal. He wants us to understand what his death did for us.

PERSONAL SALVATION

In addition to believing that Jesus died for the sin of humanity, we must also be convinced that Jesus died for each one of us. Salvation from our sin is hinged to the awareness that Jesus saved us from what we deserved. In other words, have we seen beyond the cosmic implications of Christ's death to consider that he had *us* in mind when he died?

In a statement that has become the most-quoted verse in the Bible, Jesus explained why he came: "For God so loved the world that He gave His only begotten Son, that whoever believes in Him should not perish but have everlasting life" (John 3:16). God loves the whole world, but what Christ's death set in place for all humanity must be embraced by each individual. Far too many people miss heaven by only eighteen inches—between head and heart. They believe in their heads that God was in Christ reconciling the world to himself, but the fact of his love never reaches their hearts to germinate as faith.

Jesus came to save us from sin. A gap exists between God and us caused by the incompatibility of his holiness and our sinfulness. Jesus bridged that gap. Because Jesus has saved us from our sins, we have access to spiritual intimacy with our Creator—the access for which we were created in the first place, the access that Adam and Eve had enjoyed before sin marred their relationship with God. Roadblocks have been removed. Detour signs have been destroyed. We can enter into a relationship with the One who created us.

PERSONAL RELATIONSHIP

What does a personal relationship with God look like? It means being aware that we have continuous access through prayer. God is always available and is always interested in what is on our minds. As we would pick up the phone to call our closest friend when we need someone to listen, so we can talk to God. No matter how busy our friend might be, our relationship is so important that he or she would drop anything, take time to listen, and help to carry our load. That's what God does. Jesus said, "Come to me, all of you who are tired and have heavy loads, and I will give you rest" (Matthew 11:28 NCV).

A personal relationship with our Creator also includes the privilege of knowing what is important to him. That means spending time in his presence listening to him. We do that by reading his Word (the Bible) and reflecting on what we've read. God really does speak to his children. Through written words preserved through the centuries, the living Lord communicates his heart. In moments of quiet when we intentionally shut out the voices and noises of the outside world, he speaks in an inaudible voice with prompting and insights. It's in these moments that we know we aren't alone. It's in these moments that we are capable of discerning direction when we are unsure of what decision to make.

PERSONAL FREEDOM

Jesus also saves us from the captivity that comes from living a self-centered life. The Savior saves us from ourselves. Simply put, this means that we no longer have to operate under the assumption that we are ultimately in charge of our lives. Not only is abdicating the "throne" of our lives a necessary action, it is a delightfully freeing one.

In his letter to the Christians in Rome, Paul acknowledged the tyranny experienced by those who have not surrendered to the lordship of Christ; they are "slaves to sin" (Romans 6:6 NCV). Slavery to sin and to ourselves may offer momentary pleasure and ego gratification, but it is hardly the freedom we were born to experience.

Now that Christ has taken residency in our hearts, we can step aside, no longer insisting on our own way. The freedom Christ gives allows us to have true life:

> But you are not ruled by your sinful selves. You are ruled by the Spirit, if that Spirit of God really lives in you. . . . So, my brothers and sisters, we must not be ruled by our sinful selves or live the way our sinful selves want. If you use your lives to do the wrong things your sinful selves want, you will die spiritually. But if you use the Spirit's help to stop doing the wrong things you do with your body, you will have true life. (Romans 8:9, 12–14 NCV)

PERSONAL SECURITY

When we appropriate in our lives the truth of what Jesus did on the cross, we are saved from having to wonder if we'll make it to heaven. The assurance of our relationship is not dependent on *our* faithfulness, but on God's. It's one thing to be saved from the fear of God's wrath; it's even better to know that we have been saved from the possibility that he might one day change his mind about calling us his children. Rest assured; that isn't possible. Otherwise, all that Jesus suffered would have been wasted.

When Jesus hung on the cross, he mustered his last ounce of dying strength to speak. "It is finished!" he cried out (John 19:30). In the original language, that expression means the full payment of an outstanding debt. The moral bankruptcy we were saddled with ceased to be a factor when the blood-soaked earth quaked at Jesus' death. His willingness to carry the sin of every person who would ever live gave God the Father the freedom to adopt us into his family forever.

Thank the Lord for his unexplainable, undeserved mercy. Thank him that you don't have to spend the rest of your life wondering if you've been good enough to get to heaven. Claim the promise of personal security:

> *Neither death, nor life, nor angels, nor ruling spirits, nothing now, nothing in the future, no powers, nothing above us, nothing below us, nor anything else in the whole world will ever be able to separate us from the love of God that is in Christ Jesus our Lord. (Romans 8:38–39 NCV)*

PERSONAL PEACE

The fact that Jesus is the Savior also means that he saves us from the need to worry about circumstances over which we have no control. In the Sermon on the Mount, Jesus made it clear that a relationship with him can result in anxiety-free living. The One who carried our cross and died for our sin says to us:

> Don't worry and say, "What will we eat?" or "What will we drink?" or "What will we wear?" The people who don't know God keep trying to get these things, and your Father in heaven knows you need them. The thing you should want most is God's kingdom and doing what God wants. Then all these other things you need will be given to you. So don't worry about tomorrow. (Matthew 6:31–34 NCV)

Isn't that wonderful? What used to be a cause for stress and worry now is a motivation for prayer. The energy we used to waste in nail-biting and hand-wringing can now be channeled into personal interaction with the One who understands what concerns us and knows what we need better than we do. Because we have direct and constant access to the Father, we've been given personal peace. Jesus promised it:

> Peace I leave with you, My peace I give to you; not as the world gives do I give to you. Let not your heart be troubled, neither let it be afraid. . . . These things I have spoken to you, that in Me you may have peace. In the world you will have tribulation; but be of good cheer, I have overcome the world. (John 14:27; 16:33)

Have you accepted Jesus as your personal Savior? Do you believe that in addition to dying for the sin of the world, he died for *your* sin? If you really don't have assurance that you have placed your hand into the scarred hand of Christ, you can. Before reading any further go back and pray the prayer on page 164.

Then begin a personal relationship with Jesus, your Savior.

Scripture Selections

❧

Nor is there salvation in any other, for there is no other name under heaven given among men by which we must be saved.

ACTS 4:12

Rejoice greatly, O daughter of Zion!
Shout, O daughter of Jerusalem!
Behold, your King is coming to you;
He is just and having salvation,
Lowly and riding on a donkey,
A colt, the foal of a donkey.

ZECHARIAH 9:9

For the Son of Man has come to save that which was lost.

MATTHEW 18:11

For there is born to you this day in the city of David a Savior, who is Christ the Lord.

LUKE 2:11

The next day John saw Jesus coming toward him, and said, "Behold! The Lamb of God who takes away the sin of the world!"

JOHN 1:29

For God so loved the world that He gave His only begotten Son, that whoever believes in Him should not perish but have everlasting life. For God did not send His Son into the world to condemn the world, but that the world through Him might be saved.

JOHN 3:16–17

Then they said to the woman, "Now we believe, not because of what you said, for we ourselves have heard Him and we know that this is indeed the Christ, the Savior of the world."

JOHN 4:42

Therefore I will look to the LORD;
I will wait for the God of my salvation;
My God will hear me.

MICAH 7:7

If you confess with your mouth the Lord Jesus and believe in your heart that God has raised Him from the dead, you will be saved. For with the heart one believes unto righteousness, and with the mouth confession is made unto salvation.

ROMANS 10:9–10

For by grace you have been saved through faith, and that not of yourselves; it is the gift of God, not of works, lest anyone should boast.

EPHESIANS 2:8–9

He is also able to save to the uttermost those who come to God through Him, since He always lives to make intercession for them.

HEBREWS 7:25

The LORD has made known His salvation;
His righteousness He has revealed in the sight of the nations.

PSALM 98:2

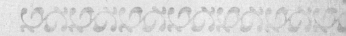

POEMS AND PRAYERS

ꚍꚍ

Beautiful Savior

Beautiful Savior, King of Creation,
Son of God and Son of Man!
Truly I'd love Thee,
Truly I'd serve Thee,
Light of my soul, my Joy, my Crown.

Fair are the meadows,
Fair are the woodlands,
Robed in flowers of blooming spring;
Jesus is fairer,
Jesus is purer,
He makes our sorrowing spirit sing.

Fair is the sunshine,
Fair is the moonlight,
Bright the sparkling stars on high;
Jesus shines brighter,
Jesus shines purer,
Than all the angels in the sky.

Beautiful Savior,
Lord of the nations,
Son of God and Son of Man!
Glory and honor,
Praise, adoration,
Now and forevermore be Thine!

—Joseph A. Seiss

Jesus, thank you for all that you have done for me. I cannot fathom such love that would suffer and die so that I might live. Thank you for saving me from my sin—and giving me a relationship with you, freedom, security, and peace. May I live a life worthy of you, my Savior. Help me never to forget what you suffered for me.

For Further Thought

ƧƆ

1. If you saw the movie *The Passion of the Christ,* describe your reactions to it.
2. How does it make you feel to think that Jesus was taking the punishment for your sin when he died on the cross?
3. Describe your personal relationship with Jesus. How does it make a difference in the way you live your life?
4. In what ways has Jesus given you personal freedom? In what ways has Jesus given you peace?

For further reflection on Jesus as your Savior, listen to "The Wonderful Cross" on the companion *Jesus* CD.

Notes

∽◌∾

JESUS, THE LORD

1. John MacArthur, *Truth for Today* (Nashville: J. Countryman, 2001), 22.
2. Ibid., 25.
3. John MacArthur, *Hard to Believe* (Nashville: Thomas Nelson Publishers, 2003), 7–8, 78–82, 86–87, 111–13.
4. MacArthur, *Truth for Today*, 49–50.

JESUS, THE MIGHTY WARRIOR

1. John Eldredge, *Waking the Dead* (Nashville: Thomas Nelson Publishers, 2003), 12–18, 95, 149–52, 163.

JESUS, THE FRIEND

1. Max Lucado, *Next Door Savior* (Nashville: W Publishing Group, 2003), 21–25, 35–40.

JESUS, THE TEACHER

1. Charles R. Swindoll, *Simple Faith* (Dallas: Word Publishing, 1991), 3–17.

JESUS, THE HEALER

1. Sheila Walsh, *The Heartache No One Sees* (Nashville: Thomas Nelson Publishers, 2004), xiii–xviii, 13–14, 70, 93–94, 106–8, 215.

JESUS, THE PRINCE OF PEACE

1. Billy Graham, *The Key to Personal Peace* (Nashville: W Publishing Group, 2003), 1-5, 41-52.

JESUS, THE LOVER OF MY SOUL

1. Dee Brestin and Kathy Troccoli, *Falling in Love with Jesus* (Nashville: W Publishing Group, 2000), 164–78.

JESUS, THE SAVIOR

1. Anne Graham Lotz, *Just Give Me Jesus* (Nashville: W Publishing Group, 2000), 262–66, 275–83.

Bible Reading Plan

৩৩

Follow these fifty-two weeks of readings to help you study
Jesus' life and ministry in one year.

Week 1
Luke 1:1–4
John 1:1–18
Matthew 1:1–17
Luke 3:23–38
Luke 1:5–25

Week 2
Luke 1:26–38
Luke 1:39–56
Luke 1:57–80
Matthew 1:18–25
Luke 2:1–7

Week 3
Luke 2:8–20
Luke 2:21–40
Matthew 2:1–12
Matthew 2:13–18
Matthew 2:19–23

Week 4
Luke 2:41–62
Luke 3:1–18
Matthew 3:13–17
Luke 4:1–13
John 1:19–28

Week 5
John 1:29–34
John 1:35–51
John 2:1–11
John 2:12–25
John 3:1–21

Week 6
John 3:22–36
Luke 3:19–20
John 4:1–26
John 4:27–38
John 4:39–42

Week 7
Matthew 4:12–17
John 4:46–54
Luke 4:16–30
Mark 1:16–20
Mark 1:21–28

Week 8
Matthew 8:14–17
Mark 1:35–39
Luke 5:1–11
Mark 1:40–45
Mark 2:1–12

Week 9
Matthew 9:9–13
Luke 5:33–39
John 5:1–18
John 5:19–30
John 5:31–47

Week 10
Matthew 12:1–8
Luke 6:6–11
Matthew 12:15–21
Mark 3:13–19
Matthew 5:1–12

Week 11
Matthew 5:13–16
Matthew 5:17–20
Matthew 5:21–26
Matthew 5:27–30
Matthew 5:31–32

Week 12
Matthew 5:33–37
Matthew 5:38–42
Matthew 5:43–48
Matthew 6:1–4
Matthew 6:5–15

Week 13
Matthew 6:16–18
Matthew 6:19–24
Matthew 6:25–34
Matthew 7:1–6
Matthew 7:7–12

Week 14
Matthew 7:13–14
Matthew 7:15–20
Matthew 7:21–29
Luke 7:1–10
Luke 7:11–17

Week 15
Luke 7:18–35
Matthew 11:20–30
Luke 7:36–50
Luke 8:1–3
Matthew 12:22–37

Week 16
Matthew 12:38–45
Mark 3:31–35
Mark 4:1–9
Mark 4:10–25
Mark 4:26–29

Week 17
Matthew 13:24–30
Matthew 13:31–32
Matthew 13:33–35
Matthew 13:36–43
Matthew 13:44

Week 18
Matthew 13:45–46
Matthew 13:47–52
Luke 8:22–25
Mark 5:1–20
Mark 5:21–43

Week 19
Matthew 9:27–34
Mark 6:1–6
Matthew 9:35–38
Matthew 10:1–16
Matthew 10:17–42

Week 20
Mark 6:14–29
John 6:1–15
Matthew 14:22–33
Matthew 14:34–36
John 6:22–40

Week 21
John 6:41–59
John 6:60–71
Mark 7:1–23
Mark 7:24–30
Mark 7:31–37

Week 22
Mark 8:1–10
Mark 8:11–13
Mark 8:14–21
Mark 8:22–26
Matthew 16:13–20

Week 23
Matthew 16:21–28
Matthew 17:1–13
Matthew 17:14–21
Matthew 17:22–23
Matthew 17:24–27

Week 24
Mark 9:33–37
Mark 9:38–41
Mark 9:42–50
Matthew 18:10–14
Matthew 18:15–20

Week 25
Matthew 18:21–35
John 7:1–9
Luke 9:51–62
John 7:10–31
John 7:32–52

Week 26
John 7:53–8:11
John 8:12–20
John 8:21–30
John 8:31–47
John 8:48–59

Week 27
Luke 10:1–16
Luke 10:17–24
Luke 10:25–37
Luke 10:38–42
Luke 11:1–13

Week 28
Luke 11:14–28
Luke 11:29–32
Luke 11:33–36
Luke 11:37–54
Luke 12:1–12

Week 29
Luke 12:13–21
Luke 12:22–34
Luke 12:35–48
Luke 12:49–53
Luke 12:54–59

Week 30
Luke 13:1–9
Luke 13:10–17
Luke 13:18–21
John 9:1–12
John 9:13–34

Week 31
John 9:35–41
John 10:1–21
John 10:22–42
Luke 13:22–30
Luke 13:31–35

Week 32
Luke 14:1–6
Luke 14:7–14
Luke 14:15–24
Luke 14:25–35
Luke 15:1–7

Week 33
Luke 15:8–10
Luke 15:11–32
Luke 16:1–18
Luke 16:19–31
Luke 17:1–10

Week 34
John 11:1–16
John 11:17–37
John 11:38–44
John 11:45–57
Luke 17:11–19

Week 35
Luke 17:20–37
Luke 18:1–8
Luke 18:9–14
Mark 10:1–12
Mark 10:13–16

Week 36
Mark 10:17–31
Matthew 20:1–16
Mark 10:32–34
Mark 10:35–45
Mark 10:46–52

Week 37
Luke 19:1–10
Luke 19:11–27
John 12:1–11
Matthew 21:1–11
Matthew 21:12–17

Week 38
John 12:20–36
John 12:37–43
John 12:44–50
Matthew 21:18–22
Matthew 21:23–27

Week 39
Matthew 21:28–32
Mark 12:1–12
Matthew 22:1–14
Matthew 22:15–22
Luke 20:27–40

Week 40
Mark 12:28–34
Mark 12:35–37
Matthew 23:1–12
Matthew 23:13–36
Matthew 23:37–39

Week 41
Mark 12:41–44
Matthew 24:1–25
Matthew 24:26–35
Matthew 24:36–51
Matthew 25:1–13

Week 42
Matthew 25:14–30
Matthew 25:31–46
Matthew 26:1–5
Luke 22:1–6
Luke 22:7–13

Week 43
John 13:1–20
Luke 22:14–30
John 13:21–30
Luke 22:31–38
John 14:1–14

Week 44
John 14:15–31
John 15:1–17
John 15:18–16:4
John 16:5–15
John 16:16–33

Week 45
John 17:1–5
John 17:6–19
John 17:20–26
Matthew 26:31–35
Mark 14:32–42

Week 46
Matthew 26:47–56
Luke 22:47–53
John 18:12–24
Matthew 26:57–68
Mark 14:66–72

Week 47
Luke 22:66–71
Matthew 27:3–10
John 18:28–37
Luke 23:1–12
Matthew 27:15–26

Week 48
John 18:38–19:16
Matthew 27:32–44
Mark 15:16–32
Luke 23:26–43
John 19:17–27

Week 49
Matthew 27:45–56
Luke 23:44–49
John 19:28–37
Mark 15:42–47
John 19:38–42

Week 50
Matthew 27:62–66
Mark 16:1–8
Luke 24:1–12
John 20:1–9
John 20:10–18

Week 51
Matthew 28:8–10
Matthew 28:11–15
Luke 24:13–35
Luke 24:36–43
John 20:24–31

Week 52
John 21:1–14
John 21:15–25
Matthew 28:16–20
Luke 24:44–49
Luke 24:50–53

Scripture Index

How well do you know Jesus?

Jesus

A Collection of Modern Worship

Reflecting the Person and Presence of Christ

Further enrich your devotional experience

with The Jesus CD...

A companion collection *of* modern worship songs

by Today's top artists.

An invitation *to* experience a closer relationship *with* Christ.

Available now wherever you buy *the* music you love!